DEMONIALITY

DEMONIALITY

LODOVICO MARIA SINISTRARI

Translated from the Latin
With an Introduction and Notes by
The Rev. Montague Summers

DOVER PUBLICATIONS, INC.
New York

Published in Canada by General Publishing Company, Ltd., 30
Lesmill Road, Don Mills, Toronto, Ontario.
Published in the United Kingdom by Constable and Company,
Ltd., 10 Orange Street, London WC2H 7EG.

This Dover edition, first published in 1989, is an unabridged and
unaltered republication of the work first published by The Fortune
Press, London, c. 1927, in an edition of 1290 copies.

Manufactured in the United States of America
Dover Publications, Inc., 31 East 2nd Street, Mineola, N.Y. 11501

Library of Congress Cataloging-in-Publication Data

Sinistrari, Lodovico Maria, 1622–1701.
 [De daemonialitate. English]
 Demoniality / Lodovico Maria Sinistrari ; translated from the Latin
with an introduction and notes by Montague Summers.
  p.   cm.
 Translation of: De daemonialitate.
 Reprint. Originally published: London : Fortune Press, 1927.
 Includes bibliographical references.
 ISBN 0-486-26147-6
 1. Demonology—Early works to 1800. 2. Catholic Church—Doctrines.
I. Summers, Montague, 1880–1948. II. Title.
BF1520.S5613   1989
133.4′23—dc20   89-39306
                                                   CIP

FOREWORD

De Dæmonialitate, et Incubis et Succubis was written during the last years of his life by Lodovico Maria Sinistrari, a famous Franciscan theologian who died 6 March, 1701. The work was not printed until 1875, when Isidore Liseux, the well-known French bibliopole, who had discovered the original manuscript in a small book-seller's shop at London in 1872, issued from his press the Latin text with a French translation, apparently made by himself, Paris, 8vo, 1875.

This version by Liseux is poor and inadequate ; he was no theologian, and he not only misunderstood many of the technical terms Sinistrari uses, but he was also unable to complete the abbreviated names of authors such as Filliucci, Francis Titelmann, Guazzo, Thomas Malvenda, and many others, to whom constant reference is made. It is worth noting that for most of the later translations from the Latin which he published Liseux employed a scholar of no little distinction, Alcide Bonneau, and therefore the collection is valuable, and a serious, indeed remarkable, contribution to literary knowledge.

In March, 1879, Liseux reprinted the De Dæmonialitate, *" Format Grand in −18," with an English transla-tion, which is something worse than indifferent. None the less, probably as being the only available English version of an important treatise, the book has become excessively rare.*

Eventually Isidore Liseux fell upon great misfortune,

v

and died in poverty 11 *January,* 1894, *at the age of fifty-eight.*

Owing to the scarcity and interest of Sinistrari's work it has been thought that a new translation would be acceptable. I would observe, however, that where there seemed to be some concise turn or happy rendering in the old translation I have not hesitated to avail myself of it in my task of englishing the Latin anew. It seemed superfluous to seek out a parallel phrase when the original was neatly expressed, and I can hardly doubt that a London friend improved certain of the pages on behalf of Liseux. Unfortunately this revision did not extend very far.

An entirely new, and, I venture to think, important feature of the present edition is that I have furnished the treatise with full notes upon such names and points as seemed to me to require that editorial attention. Without such a critical apparatus the work to all save a trained and professed theologian must lose the greater part of its value, and, what is more material, is capable of being taken in a very wrong sense.

It only remains to say that the De Dæmonialitate *is a significant expansion, ample and trebly copious no doubt, but none the less an expansion, of the article* Dæmonialitas *from the encyclopædic* De Delictis et Pœnis, Titulus Quartus ; De Delictis contra Castitatem, XIII. ; *pp.* 249–254, *ed. Romæ, folio, Giannini,* 1754.

INTRODUCTION

Lodovico Maria Sinistrari, of the Order of Reformed Minors of the Strict Observance of S. Francis, was born on the 26 February, 1622, at Ameno, a small town some few miles from Orta, in the diocese of Novara, Piedmont, a suffragan of Vercelli, during the episcopate of Carlo Bescapé, a Barnabite, who is honourably known in letters as the elegant and learned historian of his see.

The young Sinistrari received a liberal education, and with great distinction pursued the course of Humanities in the ancient University of Pavia, which even in Roman times was a literary centre ; and, later, as the capital of the Lombard kingdom boasted its " grammar " schools, whilst the Emperor Lothair erected a " college " there in 825. Pavia, famous in every branch of scholarship, especially excelled in Roman Law, even rivalling (her sons declared) the proud Bologna. The professors were often religious, as, for example, the Servite Filippo Ferrari (1646), a mathematician of no mean renown, whose lectures Sinistrari most probably attended ; and Fra Giovanni Battista Drusiano of the same Marian Order, who was the first to teach military architecture (1645), and who assisted so nobly in the defence of the city when it was besieged by the French during 1655.

Eminent doctors filled the Chairs of Theology and Philosophy, whilst Astrology had been taught at Pavia since the year 1374. In Sinistrari's day the great reputation of Gerolamo Cordano, naturalist and occult astrologer (died 1576), was yet green.

In the year 1647 Sinistrari entered the Order of Franciscans. No doubt in his boyhood he had come under the gentle influence of the Franciscan Fathers of Miasino, where there is a famous convent of the Greyfriars, yet visited by the traveller if only for the sake of the fine sunset view of Monte Rosa which may be thence obtained. Hard by his native Orta, also, is the Sacro Monte, a sanctuary dedicated to the stigmatized Patriarch of Assisi, a retreat beautifully situated upon a well-wooded promontory, approached by some twenty chapels or oratories, where the sweetly languorous magnolia and the tropical cactus bloom amid open gardens in fullest luxuriance and florid loveliness.

Acting under the shrewd direction of his Superiors Sinistrari now applied himself with whole-hearted intenseness to pedagogics and the practice of tuition. So keen a psychologist as he soon excelled in these infinitely difficult, but most profoundly human, acquirements, and he was shortly nominated Professor of Philosophy at Pavia. After a little while he proceeded to a yet more onerous task, and for fifteen years he taught Theology to the admiration and applause of Italy's most learned masters and scholars. His lecture room was crowded month after month by throngs of students who were attracted from all parts of Europe owing to his high repute and the fame of his encyclopædic knowledge.

At the same time he preached courses of Lenten and Advent sermons in many of the principal cities of Italy. The cathedrals, when he occupied the pulpit, never failed to be filled from end to end with multitudes who hung upon his sacred eloquence, whilst the Missions which he held in country towns and even in smaller villages, for he deemed no labour of the priesthood to be unworthy of his utmost care, reaped their own reward, a rich harvest of glowing piety and innumerable conversions.

A scrupulously exact religious, he was none the less an urbane and cultured man of the world. His fine bearing and courteous manners made him as agreeable at the sumptuous table of prelates and princes as at the humble and scantier board of the refectory and convent cenaculum.

In person he is described as being well-built and athletic, with a singularly graceful gait, tall, of an open and comely countenance, with a high, broad forehead, bright lively hazel eyes that flashed with intellect, and a somewhat ruddy complexion.

His conversation was remarkable for its easy sallies of wit, whereby he could attract and hold the attention of the most desultory or careless listener, and awaken a yet warmer enthusiasm in the heart of the devoted and eager scholar. Among his companions of the cloister he was, moreover, remarkable for a very real devotion and a truly humble spirit, which enabled him to sustain without any fretful complaints or grum parade of mortification, but with unconquerable patience and a placid composure, frequent attacks of gout that severely tormented him, sufferings which were far from relieved by his constant study and ceaseless labours, often protracted into the midnight hours after a long day of almost unbroken academic toil. His contemporaries, indeed, especially noted the mildness of his temper, his candour, and, so his brethren tell us, the perfect observance of his religious rule in every minutest particular.

He was in truth, as they loved to call him, omnium scientiarum uir. *Such leisure moments, or, rather, such rare respite as he allowed himself from his unwearied research into profounder authors, he gave to the study of languages other than his own, many of which he mastered without the help of any formal teacher, reading them with great facility, and even speaking them with fluency and precision, and, so keen was his ear, he was acknowledged by the native professors of the several tongues to be gifted with a singularly pure accent and enunciation.*

The writings of Sinistrari are amply sufficient to prove that not only was he deeply versed in theology and philosophy, but also that he had no superficial acquaintance with both Greek and Latin classics, since from time to time he will cite, or give a reference to, some passage, some unique word, from one of the obscurer poets or historians, and by this rare analogue he will throw a whole flood of light upon the modern custom, incident, or circumstance of which he is immediately treating. As a Latinist his reputation should stand high. In the main, the subjects of which he treats, articles of faith, canons, moral complexes, their understanding and their solution, do not admit of any studied elegance of phrase or recondite, if brilliant, flowers of oratory. The best style a theologian may boast is conciseness, clarity, and correctness. Sinistrari can show all these to a very remarkable extent. But when opportunity is given—and occasion does not unseldom arise—for him to relate some personal experience touching the matter under debate, to recount some history which is not impertinent, then may we recognize that he does possess a power of narration which is enhanced by such literary graces that the essayist, the novelist, and the writer upon profaner subjects might profitably both imitate and admire. Had Sinistrari not devoted his attention so particularly to the highly technical principles and practices of Civil and Canon law, he would no doubt have won laurelled distinction among the literary and æsthetic Academies of the day, of which, as it may be remembered, perhaps the most famous of all, the Arcadi, held their first solemn gathering, 5 October, 1690, on the Gianicolo, in a bosky wood belonging to the Reformed Minorites, his own brethren in the religious family.

Sinistrari was a poet of rare felicities. We may point to the exquisite picture he has drawn of his own native countryside; the blithe hamlet of Ameno, the lake of sapphire-blue, the snow-capped mountains beyond, the fair church and gay villas of the Isola di San Giulio that rise, as it were, from the very bosom of the waters, the glimmering woods, among which are emparadised the white walls and reverend belfries of ancient monastery and gentle cloister, of lone sanctuary and pensive hermitage. He uses the flexible Latin words with a delicacy that is almost a caress, moulding, as only a master may, in lyric harmonies of sweetest cadence those fondling diminutives which Catullus, and, above all, Pontano, loved. I am reminded of the poets of the silver Renaissance, of Ottavio's charming Ad Iuliam, of Averano's Ad Amicum Rusticantem, of the Neapolitan Bernardino Rota, of Sicci, Favorito, Fabio Segni, Maschiano, Virginio Cesarini, Baldinotti, Maffio Barberini, and a dozen more. One finds in Sinistrari with added loveliness the simple beauty and genuine feeling of those lines of Flaminio, Ad Agellum Suum,

*which almost seem some waif of the Anthology, some scat-
tered page from a Latin Longus :—*

> Umbræ frigidulæ, arborum susurri,
> Antra roscida, discolore picta
> Tellus gramine, fontium loquaces
> Lymphæ, garrula aues, amica Musis
> Otia : o mihi si uolare uestrum
> In sinum superi annuant benigni :
> Si dulci liceat frui recessu,
> Et nunc ludere uersibus iocosis,
> Nunc somnum uirides sequi per umbras,
> Nunc mulgere manu mea capellam,
> Lacteoque liquore membra sicca
> Irrigare per æstum, et æstuosis
> Curis dicere plurimam salutem :
> O quæ tunc mihi uita, quam beata,
> Quam uitæ similis foret deorum !

It was hardly possible that so famous a scholar should
not soon attract the notice of the highest authorities, and
accordingly we are not surprised to find that Sinistrari was
summoned to Rome to fill the position of Consultor to the
Supreme Tribunal of the Most Holy Inquisition. The
chief official of this Congregation is the Commissarius
Sancti Officii, *a Dominican of the Lombard province, and
there can be no doubt that it was owing to the Commissioner
of the day, who, coming from Lombardy, must have known
Sinistrari well, that this important appointment was
made.*

The Holy Office is the first among the Roman Congre-
gations. It was introduced by Pope Paul III., 1542,
although Sixtus V., by his Constitution Immensa
Æterni, 22 January, 1587, may be regarded as the real
organiser of the Supreme Tribunal. The Holy Office includes judges, officials, consultors, and qualificators, all
posts of the first importance and responsibility.

The judges are cardinals nominated by the Pope, and their actual number depends on his will. It may be noticed that this congregation differs from all others, inasmuch as it has no Cardinal-prefect : the Pope himself is Prefect of the Holy Office, and he always presides in person when a momentous decision is to be pronounced (coram Sanctissimo). *On Mondays there takes place, at the palace of the Holy Office, a meeting of the Consultors, whose duty it is to afford the cardinals expert advice and bring forward seasonable recommendations. They are very often from the secular clergy, but the General of the Dominicans, the* magister sacri palatii *and a third member of the same Order are always ex-officio consultors* (consultores nati). *The qualificators are appointed for life indeed, yet they only give their opinions when called upon to do so with reference to some particular point. The Holy Office has jurisdiction over all Christians.*

For some years Sinistrari acted as Vicar-General to the Archbishop of Avignon, whose see comprises the territory embraced by the department of Vaucluse. The prelate in question, whose episcopate lasted from 1673–84, *was Hyacinth Libelli of Tiferno, O.P., Master of the Sacred Palace to Clement X.* " *Non in theologia tantum sed in omnia quoque scientiarum genere fuit uersatissimus," says Sainte Marthe. Sinistrari was appointed as a coadjutor to Claude Pertuyse, now an old man, worn out and broken with some thirty years of ceaseless anxiety and gravest responsibility. This was then no enviable position, but an outpost needing the continual exercise of the nicest tact and most skilful diplomacy. The Houses of Valois and Bourbon had more than once endeavoured to subject the papal territory to the French crown, and in 1663 Louis XIV., in consequence of an unfortunate attack made upon the mohocking attendants of the overbearing and arrogant Duc de Créqui, his ambassador at Rome, swooped down upon Avignon, which was forthwith declared an integral part of the realm of France by the jingoistic Parliament of Provence. Nor was the sequestration raised until Flavio Chigi, the Cardinal Padrone, nephew of Alexander VII., had tendered an ample apology. In 1688, during the reign of the Venerable Innocent XI., another French attempt at the sudden occupation of Avignon was made, but without success. By this time, however, Sinistrari had long left the troublous Archdiocese, and after a short residence again in Rome was acting as Theologian to Federico Caccia, the Cardinal-Archbishop of Milan.*

From Rome, where he could find no leisure owing to the constant press of visitors, many of whom being of noble birth and highest rank, both ecclesiastical and lay, could not be denied, Sinistrari had withdrawn to the Franciscan retreat of the Sacro Monte, hoping that here he might complete his great work De Delictis et Pœnis *undisturbed. Of his native convent he has left us a charming picture :* " Collis molliter accliuis est, cuius iugo, quod muralis clausuræ corona cingit, incubat Conuentus qui mirabili undique gaudet prospectu. . . . A Septentrione curuati in arcum uisuntur colliculi, uitibus frutetisque consiti, quibus subiecta planities, pratis, campis, syluisque distincta in gremio excipit Oppidum, cui ex situs amœnitate Ameni uocabulum inditum est." *But the summons to Milan forced him back into the busy world. A year's illness also intervened, and it was only by dint of sheer dogged work and hours stolen from sleep that he was able to put the finishing touches to his noble volume.*

At the suggestion of José Ximenes Santiago, who, upon his retirement in 1682 from the office of Minister-General of the Franciscan Order, had been obliged by Innocent XI. to accept the mitre as Bishop of Placentia, the plenary Chapter of Franciscans which met in 1688, entrusted Sinistrari with the compilation of the statutes of the Order. This formidable task he performed in his treatise entitled Practica criminalis Minorum illustrata. *Ever a student and lover of books, pen in hand to the last, he died in the pontificate of Clement XI. on 6 March, 1701, at the ripe old age of seventy-nine, honoured and regretted by all.*

His several tractates were more than once reprinted early in the eighteenth century, and his complete works have been collected, 3 vols., folio, 1753–1754: R. P. Ludovici Mariæ Sinistrari de Ameno Opera omnia, Romæ, in domo Caroli Gianniani. *Herein are included the* Practica criminalis Minorum illustrata ; Formularium criminale ; De incorrigibilium expulsione ab Ordinibus Regularibus ; *and the* De Delictis et Pœnis.

The De Dæmonialitate, *the manuscript of which was discovered in London in 1872, was printed for the first time in the year 1875.*

When we consider how acute and how accurate a theologian Sinistrari was, how great was his fame during his lifetime, and what high positions he held with credit and applause both at the University of Pavia and at the Roman Court, it will come as something of a surprise to many to learn that one of his books, or rather the first edition of one of his books, was actually placed upon the Index. It must at once be pointed out that the Index librorum prohibitorum *is a highly technical codex or catalogue, and that, generally speaking, books are only included therein for highly technical reasons. The curious inquirer who imagines that he has got hold of a guide to knowledge in the shape of a copious list of those volumes which booksellers of the meaner sort are apt to dub " Facetiæ," that is to say undiluted pornography, when he eagerly turns the pages of the Index will be most woefully and grievously disappointed. Instead of salacious titles to thrill his jaded fancy with some new arcana of phallism, instead of lewdness and lubricity, he will read long columns of dusty names of dead and gone heresiarchs, men whose works have left not an echo behind them, he will read the dreary captions of Lethean volumes, " Dry Bodies of Divinity," of pseudophilosophy, whose pages have gone to wrap up as many mackerel and bloaters as did the* Annals of Volusius *in ancient* Rome *long centuries ago.*

Yet on the Index is filed : Sinistrari (Ludovicus Maria) de Ameno, De Delictis et Pœnis Tractatus absolutissimus. Donec corrigatur. Decret. 4 Martii, 1709. Correctus autem iuxta editionem Romanam anni 1753 permittitur.

The De Delictis et Pœnis *was published for the first time at* Venice *in* 1700, Venetiis, apud Hieronymum Albricium, MDCC. *It is a treatise, extraordinarily complete, dealing with all imaginable crimes, sins, and offences ; and in most cases it discusses the punishment due to the crime, the penalties inflicted both by the ecclesiastical and by the civil law.*

The closing decades of the seventeenth century were a time of great and perplexing intellectual difficulties. In Moral Theology Rigorists (even Jansenists), Probabilists, Aequiprobabilists, Probabiliorists, and Laxists were putting forward conflicting views ; they contended for their opinions with the utmost pertinacity, and it is hardly to be wondered at that, in their revolt from the bitter severities of Port-Royal, the spiritual harshness, and the pessimism which, however unintentionally, none the less inevitably, this narrow attitude of mind was bound to produce, some few theologians went perhaps a thought too far in the opposite direction.

As early as 1653 Innocent X. condemned the five propositions which had been taken from the Augustinus, published after the death of its author, Jansen, folio, 1640, and another blow was dealt at rigorism in 1657 by Alexander VII., but this school did not seem absolutely forbidden and completely banned until 1690, when Alexander VIII. in uncompromising and directest terms condemned the proposition of Sinnichius, a leading rigorist : Non licet sequi opinionem uel inter probabiles probabilissimam. *On the other hand, for fear of the least shadow of scandal the Popes corrected certain tendencies of Laxism, and thus we find that many leading authorities were in some small points impugned by the punctilious vigilance of Innocent XI. and Alexander VII. Accordingly there were censured propositions which had been speculatively approved by the Theatine Antonio Diana (died 1663), a Consultor of the Holy Office of the Kingdom of Sicily and an examiner of Bishops ; theorems advanced by the famous and learned Juan Caramuel (died 1682), sometime Archbishop of Otranto ; by the profound theologian Leander (died 1663) ; by Juan Azor, S.J. (died 1603) ;*

by De Graphæis ; and by not a few other authoritative names. Nay, more, important books were actually forbidden. Thus the famous Aphorismi Confessariorum ex Uariis Doctorum Sententiis collecti, *published Venice,* 1595, *of Manoel de Sa, S.J. (died* 1596), *who for his holy life was held in high honour by Pope S. Pius V., was placed on the Index in* 1603, *and only removed in* 1900. (*For a quarter of a century I have constantly used the* Aphorismi, Coloniæ, sumptibus Petri Amorfortii MDXCIX., *with the approbation of the Censor Silvester Pardo, a Canon of Antwerp, and I should indeed find it difficult to say why this treatise had merited a censure.*)

Two works of the great Etienne Bauny, S.J., who died in the odour of sanctity 1649, Practique du droit canonique au gouvernment de l'Église, *Paris,* 1634, *and* De Sacramentis ac Personis Sacris . . . Theologiæ moralis pars prima, *Paris, folio,* 1640, *are both on the Index. What seems perhaps even more remarkable, is that by a decree of* 4 *February,* 1627, *there were placed on the Index some editions of Volume III. of the* Disputationes de sancti Matrimonii Sacramento, *first published* 1602–3, *the famous work of Thomas Sanchez, S.J., who died in* 1610. *But displeasure was caused by his treatment of a highly technical point, the power of the Pope to grant a valid legitimation of the offspring of marriages gravely invalid under Canon Law ; Book VIII., disputatio* 7. *It is perhaps worth noting that Sanchez also upholds a theory concerning mental reservation, which was the twenty-sixth thesis condemned by Innocent XI.*

Since the Supreme Authority from time to time deemed it expedient that in some small point so many and such great writers should have been corrected, it is no real reflection upon the sound erudition and orthodoxy of Sinistrari that on account of some formal small circumstance, a certain numerical ambiguity to wit in one or two paragraphs, his De Delictis et Pœnis *should have been censured. Moreover, it was not until nine years after his death that any fault was alleged, and even then the mitigating rubric* Donec corrigatur, " *Until such time as it be amended,*" *was added; although this, of course, was beyond the author's power.*

I would emphasize, and emphasize most particularly, that no disapprobation was ever expressed of his work on Demoniality, the doctrine of which, however fantastic it may appear, however singular, we are not called upon to reprobate and damn as impossible. We are not in any way bound to subscribe thereto ; the theories of Sinistrari may not commend themselves to us ; we may deem them in the highest degree improbable ; but we must not say that they are unthinkable and inconceivable. We should bear in mind the sage words of Pliny, Historia Naturalis, *VII.,* 1 : " *Quemadmodum multa fieri non posse, priusquam facta sunt, iudicantur : ita multa quoque, quæ antiquitus facta, quia nos ea non uidimus, neque ratione assequimur, ex iis esse, quæ fieri non potuerunt, iudicamus. Quæ certe summa insipientia est.*"

The title of this curious tractate is Demoniality, *and it will not be impertinent to inquire into the exact sense in which Sinistrari uses this word. In the first place, the* New English Dictionary, Oxford, 1897, *Vol. III.,* has, " Demoniality (rare). *The nature of demons ; the realm of demons, demons collectively. (Cf.* spirituality.)"

The title of the present work is then cited with date 1879, *"first English translation." The second quotation runs as follows: "* 1891. Saturday Review, 2 May, 543/2. *The old wives' fables . . . are those of demoniality, black masses, etc." It must be confessed that the meaning given by the* New English Dictionary *is sufficiently vague, although at the same time all inclusive. It would, moreover, be a difficult, perhaps impossible, task to find an exact and conciser definition. Sinistrari is careful to explain his terms at the outset, and it is well that he is at some trouble to do so, for the Incubi and Succubi of whom he treats are by no means to be conceived in the ordinary acceptance of these words, that is to say, as devils from the pit, utterly evil and malign, but rather as spiritual beings of a mixed nature, by no means necessarily baleful and infernal, although light and wanton enough, for, as Dom Calmet says, in his* Traité sur les Apparitions des Esprits, *third edition, "* revûe, corrigée & augmentée par l'Auteur," *Paris,* 1751, *tome I., p.* 248 : *" Ces Esprits ne sont pas malfaisans, à moins qu'on ne les insulte, & qu'on ne se moque d'eux : car alors ils se mettent de mauvaise humeur, ils jettent quelque chose à ceux qui les outragent."*

The word Demon, too, is often used by Sinistrari, not as meaning fiend, cacodemon, but almost in the sense of the Greek word δαίμων, *which term itself had many shades of difference in its signification. By Homer, for example, it is interchanged with* θεός, *so in* Odyssey, VI., 172–164 :

νῦν δ'ἐνθάδε κάββαλε δαίμων
ὄφρ' ἔτι που καὶ τῇδε πάθω κακόν. οὐ γάρ ὀίω
παύσεσθ'· ἀλλ'ἔτι πολλὰ θεοὶ τελέουσι πάροιθεν.

Apparently Apuleius took the word in practically the same sense, for he calls his treatise which discusses the δαίμων of Socrates, De Deo Socratis Liber, *and Thomas Taylor the Platonist, in a note, says :* " *As the dæmon of Socrates, therefore, was doubtless one of the highest order, as may be inferred from the intellectual superiority of Socrates to most other men, Apuleius is justified in calling this dæmon a God."* *However* θεός *is never used for* δαίμων, *though* δαίμων *is for* θεός.

The dæmones formed the connecting link between gods and men, but, especially in the Greek tragedians the dæmon may be bad, and Æschylus, Agamemnon 1569, *in a speech of Clytæmnestra, uses the word of the evil genius of the whole family :*

ἐγὼ δ' οὖν
ἐθέλω δαίμονι τῷ Πλεισθενιδῶν
ὅρκους θεμένη τάδε μὲν στέργειν,
δύστλητά περ ὄνθ'·

In New Testament Greek δαίμων, *is equivalent to an evil spirit, a devil.*

The thesis which Sinistrari sets forth in detail may be stated as follows : There are in existence on earth rational creatures besides man, endowed like him with a body and a soul ; they are born and die like him ; they are redeemed by Our Lord Jesus Christ, and therefore are capable of being saved or being lost. These rational creatures or animals are swayed by the same emotions and passions, jealousies and lusts, as man. They are affected by material substances ; therefore they participate in the matter of those substances, that is to say, they have corporeity. But this corporeity is far more tenuous and subtile than the body of a man. It enjoys a certain rarity, permea-

bility, volatility, and power of sublimation. These crea-
tures are able at will to withdraw themselves from the sight
of man.

We find that Our Lord in His human body made use of
this power as is recorded by S. Luke, iv. 16–30, *who tells*
us that when He had preached in the Synagogue at Nazareth
" *all they in the Synagogue, hearing these things, were filled*
with anger. And they rose up and thrust Him out of the
city; and they brought Him to the brow of the hill,
whereon their city was built, that they might cast Him
down headlong. But He, passing through the midst of
them, went His way." Ipse autem transiens per
medium illorum, ibat. *Which is to say that Our Lord*
withdrew Himself from their sight, made Himself in-
visible. The Saints also have been able to exercise this
power. Queen Yolanda of Aragon, the wife of Juan I.,
1387–95, *during the residence of S. Vincent Ferrer at*
Salamanca, 1391–5, *had chosen the great Dominican for*
her director, and, on one occasion, she expressed a desire to
visit the enclosure, which the saint refused. However,
relying upon her royal privilege, she forced her way into the
monastery, where she was informed that S. Vincent had
retired to his own room. She entered; but the holy father
was nowhere to be seen, nor could he be found anywhere
throughout the whole house. When she had departed, in
bitter and voluble disappointment, one of the friars repair-
ing to S. Vincent's room found him seated there engaged in
study. "Where have you been, my father?" asked the
friar in astonishment. "Why did you not meet the
Queen?" The saint replied in tones of sternest rebuke :
" *As for me, I was here the whole time. I have not*

stirred. But no woman shall come to my room to see me, not even the Queen. God will punish her sorely for her intrusion." And such, indeed, proved to be the case until Yolanda had humbly sought for pardon, and was forgiven by this great son of S. Dominic.

S. Francis of Paula, having courageously rebuked Ferdinand I. of Naples for his violation of ecclesiastical rights, the tyrant sent a company of sixty soldiers to seize the saint. He, however, remained quietly in prayer before the high altar, and although the royal halberdiers made a thorough search of the whole convent and chapel, and even touched the saint, they were unable to see him, and so, willy-nilly, returned empty handed to their master.

These Incubi, of whom Sinistrari speaks, have also the cognate power of passing through material objects, that is to say, they are able to enter a room, or a house, the doors of which are locked and closed. This mystic phenomenon is not uncommon in the lives of the saints. It is recorded, for example, of S. Dominic and of S. Rita the Augustinian. In the Annals of the Friars Preachers *we are told that Blessed Maurice was one day passing the night in the cottage of the sacristan of Waizen in Hungary. The host, happening to enter his guest's chamber, and not finding him, became alarmed, more especially as he was no longer anywhere on the premises. The church itself had been closed for some hours and all the doors secured, but there eventually Blessed Maurice was discovered, plunged in prayer. Clara d'Agolanto, who founded the convent of the Holy Angels at Rimini, was wont to retire to the chapel and pass many hours in penitential exercises whilst the rest were slumbering and asleep. At length the sisters, fearing that she might suffer from excess of zeal, as they deemed it, took the precaution of locking the doors to prevent her from entering the cold midnight sanctuary. Nevertheless, on the following evening, although the keys had never left the charge of the portress, the holy Clara, by some extraordinary miracle, had passed through the intervening barriers, and was, as usual, performing her acts of mortification before the tabernacle.*

Sinistrari's thesis, then, does not set forth any new and novel phenomena, but only attributes known, if extremely exceptional, powers to these rational creatures whom he calls Incubi. And it is beyond dispute that if they do exist, they do possess the qualities which he has invested them with, and assigned to them. In reading Sinistrari we must be, before all else, scrupulously careful continually to bear in mind his exact definition of, and the precise meaning he gives to, the word Incubus. *Commonly speaking, we employ the word Incubus to mean a demon, a witch's familiar, who, as S. Augustine says,* De Ciuitate Dei, *XV.,* 23, *are truly devils, that* " *have often injured women, desiring and acting carnally with them.*"

Guazzo, in his Compendium Maleficarum, Milan, 1608, *I.,* 7, *says, with reference to these demons :* " *This familiar can assume either a male or a female shape; sometimes he appears as a full-grown man, sometimes as a satyr; and if it is a woman who has been received as a witch he generally assumes the form of a rank buck-goat.*" *S. Thomas,* Summa, Pars Prima, *quæstio I., a.* 3, *et* 6, *and S. Bonaventura,* Sententiarum, Liber II., d. viii. Pars Prima, a. 3, q.l., *both assert the existence of incubi who are demons. A vast library of other authorities might be quoted. It will be sufficient to cite S. Alphonsus Liguori, who in his* Praxis confessariorum, *VII., n.* 111, *writes :* " *Some deny that there are evil spirits, incubi and succubi ; but writers of weight, eminence, and learning, for the most part lay down that such is verily the case."* Charles-René Billuart, *the celebrated Dominican* (1685–1757), *in his* Tractatus de Angelis *expressly declares :* " *The same evil spirit may serve as a succubus to a man, and as an incubus to a woman." So, in general acceptance, the Incubus is a demon, and more precisely a demon employed for the purpose of fornicating with witches.*

Now the Incubus, as Sinistrari uses the term, and as in studying his treatise we must understand it, is not a demon, but he is a lutin—*there seems to be no exact English term to express him as Sinistrari conceives him. He is frequently mischievous and vexatious ; not unseldom rampant and lickerish ; a whoremaster, neighing after copulation ; but not demoniacal. It should be remarked that the title* Demoniality *is itself apt to be entirely misleading, for the treatise is not immediately concerned with devils, but with these* lutins. *Here, again, we can only say that there is no English term to convey the precise meaning Sinistrari has assigned to the Latin* Dæmonialitas, *and any new coinage is (I think) altogether to be avoided.*

It is quite probable that with the passage of time these incubi have greatly decreased in number, and therefore are much less in evidence. In olden days there were possibly more frequent manifestations, and the legends of that time when " *Al was this land fulfild of fayerye " may have, far back in the remotest centuries, more solid foundation than we are willing or apt to allow.*

The prophet Isaias (xxxiv. 14), speaking of a desolate land, says : " Erit cubile draconum, et pascua struthionum. Et occurrent dæmonia onocentauris, et pilosus clamabit alter ad alterum : ibi cubauit lamia, et inuenit sibi requiem." " And it shall be the habitation of dragons, and the pasture of ostriches. And demons and monsters shall meet, and the hairy ones shall cry out one to another, there hath the lamia lain down, and found rest for herself " (Douay). " And it shall be an habitation of dragons, and a court for owls. The wild beasts of the desert shall also meet with the wild beasts of the island, and the satyr shall cry to his fellow ; the screech owl also shall rest there, and find for herself a place of rest " (A.V. with marginal note on " screech owl " : Or, night-monster). " And it shall be an habitation of jackals, a court for ostriches. And the wild beasts of the desert shall meet with the wolves, and the satyr shall cry to his fellow ; yea, the night-monster shall settle there, and shall find her a place of rest " (R.V. with marginal note on " the night-monster " : Heb. Lilith). S. Jerome in his gloss says : " Pilosi, uel Incubones, uel Satyros : siluestres quosdam homines, quos nonulli Faunos Ficarios uocant." It may well be that in this passage the satyr and lamia refer to some very degenerate and lower incubi.

It has been suggested that the demi-gods of Greece and Rome, satyrs, fauns, silvans, pans, nymphs, oreads, hamadryads, and all the vast company of nature-deities, were, in truth, these incubi and succubi. It is not impertinent to remark in this connexion that in later days from the time of the Satyr of Praxiteles (born circa 390 B.C.) *the type tends to become even handsome, and the satyrs are represented as comely youths with nothing of an animal form save the pointed ears, and, it may be, the luxuriant hair. But they are always excessively wanton, as is so often the case with the incubi. This identification certainly seems to receive support from the history of S. Antony the Great, who died* 356–357, *and who, when on his way to visit S. Paul the Hermit, met in the desert a satyr. And the satyr bowed down before him, and said :* " *I am one of those creatures who haunt the woods and fields and remote places, and who are worshipped by the blind pagans as Gods. Yet thou knowest we are mortal, and I am come to beseech thee that thou wouldst pray for me, interceding for me and my people, to thy God, who is my God, and the God of all creation." This account we receive from S. Jerome, whose authority is, of course, final and indisputable. Nay, more, the holy Doctor, whilst allowing that the incident is very extraordinary, avers and affirms that it is true. He emphatically adds :* " *Hoc ne cuiquam ad incredulitatem scrupulum moueat, sub rege Constantio, uniuerso mundo teste, defenditur. Nam Alexandriam istiusmodi homo uiuus perductus magnum populo spectaculum præbuit : et postea cadauer exanime, ne calore æstatis dissiparetur, sale infuso, Antiochiam ut ab Imperatore uideretur, allatum est,"* Uita S. Pauli, primi eremitae, viii. (*Migne :* P. L., *Vol.* XXIII., 23–24). *One may compare Eutropius, Lib.* XII., *and S. Isidore, Lib.* IX., Originum. *Heraclitus* De Incredibilibus, *c.* 25, *asserts that there dwelt in the mountains strange beings,* τράγωνδε τρῖχας καὶ σκελὴ ἔχειν.

Plutarch tells us that at Dyrrhachium, in Greek Illyria, Sulla once saw a satyr ; Uita Sullæ, XXVII. 3 :

" Ἐνταῦθά φασι κοιμώμενον ἁλῶναι σάτυρον, οἷον οἱ πλάσται καὶ γραφεῖς ἐικάζουσιν, ἀχθέντα δὲ ὡς Σύλλαν ἐρωτᾶσθαι δι' ἑρμηνέων πολλῶν, ὅστις ἔιη· φθεγξαμένου δε μόλις οὐδὲν συνετῶς, ἀλλὰ τραχειάν τινα καὶ μάλιστα μεμιγμένην ἵππου τε χρεμετισμῷ καὶ τράγου μηκασμῷ φωνὴν ἀφέντος, ἐκπλαγέντα τόν Σύλλαν ἀποδιοπομπήσασθαι."

I have already hinted that many of the old fairy legends of England, of Ireland, and, indeed, of all Western countries, may have owed something of their source to the apparitions, the vagaries, and the loves of the incubi. This was in the old heathen days, before S. Augustine came. The incubi fled away when the Holy Catholic Church was established in these Isles, as the grey twilight vanishes in the radiant glories of the rising sun. Poets have fancifully lamented over their departure, and sweetly sung their trentals. The Father of English poetry himself has elegized them in a strain of surpassing beauty :—

> *In th' olde dayes of the king Arthour,*
> *Of which that Britons speken greet honour,*
> *Al was this land fulfild of fayerye.*
> *The elf-queen, with hir joly companye,*
> *Daunced ful ofte in many a grene mede ;*
> *This was the olde opinion, as I rede.*
> *I speke of manye hundred yeres ago ;*
> *But now can no man see none elves mo.*
> *For now the grete charitee and prayeres*
> *Of limitours and othere holy freres,*
> *That serchen every lond and every streem,*
> *As thicke as motes in the sonne-beem,*
> *Blessinge halles, chambres, kichenes, boures,*
> *Citees, burghes, castels, hye toures,*
> *Thropes, bernes, shipnes, dayeryes,*
> *This maketh that ther been no fayeryes.*

For ther as wont to walken was an elf,
Ther walketh now the limitour himself
In undermeles and in morweninges,
And seyth his matins and his holy thinges
As he goth in his limitacioun.
Wommen may go saufly up and doun,
In every bush, or under every tree ;
Ther is noon other incubus but he,
And he ne wol doon hem but dishonour.

*Ireland is still the happy haunt of fairies. As Mr.
W. B. Yeats has related :* " *There are some doubters
even in the western villages. One woman told me last
Christmas that she did not believe either in hell or in
ghosts. Hell was an invention got up by the priests to
keep people good ; and ghosts would not be permitted, she
held, to go* ' *trapsing about the earth* ' *at their own free
will ;* ' *but there are faeries and little leprechauns, and
water-horses, and fallen angels.* ' *I have met also a man
with a Mohawk Indian tattooed upon his arm, who held
exactly similar beliefs and unbeliefs. No matter what
one does, one never doubts the faeries, for, as the man with
the Mohawk Indian on his arm said,* ' *they stand to
reason.* ' " *Surely these faeries and little leprechauns, and
other Irish pixies, sprites, kobolds, and goblins, are none
other than the incubi of whom Sinistrari speaks. Myself,
I firmly believe in their existence and in these appearances.
There is nothing here contrary to philosophers and Catholic
theology, and S. Augustine bears me out and confirms this
conviction.*

Again, Mr. Yeats records : " *One day I was walking
over a bit of marshy ground close to Inchy Wood when I
felt, all of a sudden, and only for a second, an emotion
which I said to myself was the root of Christian mysticism.*

. . . A few nights after this I awoke to see the loveliest people I have ever seen. A young man and a young girl dressed in olive-green raiment, cut like old Greek raiment, were standing at my bedside. I looked at the girl and noticed that her dress was gathered about her neck into a kind of chain, or perhaps into some kind of stiff embroidery which represented ivy-leaves. But what filled me with wonder was the miraculous mildness of her face. There are no such faces now. It was beautiful, as few faces are beautiful, but it had neither, one would think, the light that is in desire or in hope or in fear or in speculation. It was peaceful, like the faces of animals, or like mountain pools at evening, so peaceful that it was a little sad." Here Mr. Yeats has exactly described an incubus and his chosen of his own race, creatures who have found happiness in their own love, who are not tempest-torn by desire, who are not very far from the kingdom of God.

It is at such moments of reverie that visions are granted to the mystic ; he realises that all about him exists and moves an unseen world manifesting itself through some rent in the veil, when our perception is less gross and less blind. That great and truly spiritual genius, Dr. Havelock Ellis, in his Impressions and Comments, 1920–23, has an illuminating passage : *" As I lay with closed eyes half asleep there appeared out of blankness on the curtain of my eyelid the vision of a beautiful anonymous feminine face, and in a few moments faded as involuntarily as it appeared. The like phenomenon is apt to happen to most people. Therefore the miracle of such creation out of seeming nothingness escapes attention. It scarcely seems worth notice save to those among us who now and then discuss hypnogogic hallucinations for the languid interest of a few psychological readers. It is only to the rare child of genius, whose vision is not dulled by familiarity, that the inexplicable marvel is apparent. Of such was Leonardo da Vinci, who, after briefly summing up the familiar wonders of our dream life, can exclaim with awe : ' Oh ! maraviglia della umana spezie ! ' " Dr. Havelock Ellis and Ludovico Maria Sinistrari would, I think, perfectly have comprehended each other's point of view.*

In the remoter and unspoiled parts of England, in the heart of Dorset, in Somersetshire, on the moors of Devon, and in Cornwall, the traditional belief in the land of faerie, in pixies, pigwidgeons and flibbertigibbets, still sensibly lingers, and here, perhaps, the incubus yet loiters awhile, and is loth to go. But civilization is afraid of him, and hastens to murmur Herrick's Spell :

> *Holy water come and bring ;*
> *Cast in salt, for seasoning :*
> *Set the brush for sprinkling :*
> *Sacred spittle bring ye hither ;*
> *Meal and it now mix together,*
> *And a little oil to either.*
> *Give the tapers here their light,*
> *Ring the saints' bell, to affright*
> *Far from hence the evil sprite.*

For, as we have already said, the incubus may be a very pestering and pothersome bogle. Perhaps he was responsible for the famous hauntings at Tedworth, where an invisible drummer tabored incessantly on his drum to the confusion of the whole household and the wonderment of all England from April, 1661, to April, 1663. He may also have been the agent of the famous Epworth phenomena ;

of the unearthly occurrences at Worksop in 1883 : the goblinry at Wem in the same year; at Peterborough in 1891 ; at Turin in 1900; at Enniscarthy in 1910 ; at Folkestone in 1917 ; not to mention the hundred other strange happenings which are recorded, but not explained.

In Ireland he is more easily recognized and better known, for there, as Mr. Yeats has told us, they " believe that all nature is full of invisible people, and that some of these are ugly or grotesque, some wicked or foolish, many beautiful beyond any one we have ever seen, and that the beautiful are not far away when we are walking in pleasant and quiet places."

The Forgetful People, as the faery people are sometimes called, often appear to be of the same size as a man, often something bigger, and not infrequently about three feet high. Regina, Regina Pigmeorum, Ueni, *cried William Lilly, the old astrologer, when he evoked the little good folk beneath the haunted oaks of Windsor Forest. An aged Irish woman once said to a lady : " There's nothing to be frightened about in faeries, Miss. Many's the time I talked to a woman myself that was a faery, or something of the sort, and no less and more than mortal anyhow. She used to come about your grandfather's house—your mother's grandfather, that is—in my young days."*

One would not venture to assert that the incubus is responsible for all these visions and appearances, but it certainly does seem, if we are to accept the thesis of Sinistrari, that he is more closely connected with Irish lore and Irish legend than has hitherto been surmised and allowed.

The incubus, as Sinistrari shows him, may be compared with the Jinns of the Arabs. For, as W. R. Smith is careful to emphasize in his The Religion of the Semites (*Edinburgh, 1889, p.* 424), *the Jinns must not be considered to be demons, the " gobelyn goynge in darknessis," as Wyclif has it,* Psalm *xc.* 6 ; *as many writers mistakenly assert. Islamic commentators distinguish between Angels, all of whom are good ; Devils, all of whom are bad ; and Jinns, some of whom are good and some bad. In the* Qu'ran, *lxxxii. intitled* The Jinns, 11, *the Jinns are represented as declaring " some of us are good and some otherwise." It should be noticed, however, that Mohammed strongly reprobated any worship or cultus of the Jinns. The first Moslem writer of any importance who denied the existence of Jinns as a mere fable was Avicenna (Abu Sina, d.* 1037). *Many Jinns dwell in remotest deserts, but the friendly Jinns frequently take up their abode in the houses of human beings. They are invisible, so that it is the result of their work, not the agent, that is seen. To them are generally ascribed strange and unaccountable happenings. When annoyed they will pelt the folk in the house with missiles and utensils, a favourite trick with the poltergeist. Sometimes they filch away clothes, food, and other objects. They eat and drink like ordinary mortals. They are male and female, they can marry, and procreate their own race. Nay, more, they can beget children on human beings, or can bear children by a human father, in which cases the offspring partakes of the nature of both parents. Even as men, the Jinns are divided into the faithful and unbelievers. Those who are good Moslems perform all duties of religion, prayer, alms, fasting during the month Ramadân, the pilgrimages to Mecca and other holy places, with as much devotion as the most religious of mortals. It will be seen that the Arabian Jinn is not very unlike Sinistrari's conception of the incubus.*

It may not be irrelevant here briefly to give two anecdotes related by Italian authors to whom Sinistrari makes no reference. Coleti, in his Energumenos dignoscendi et liberandi . . . ratio *(p. 118), has devoted a chapter to the folletti. He says that we should avoid any sort of intercourse or commerce with them when they make their presence first known in a house by various silly pranks and idle japeries. Trinkets and knicknacks belonging to the house, and more especially to the person whose attention the lutin wishes to attract, vanish from the place where they had been laid down, only to reappear shortly afterwards in another spot. These tricksters next annoy people by hiding in dark corners and laughing suddenly, or calling aloud as one passes ; they will even pluck the sheets off the bed from sleepers, or tweak one's nightcap. Yet they do not seek to possess those whom they pester thus, they are merely endeavouring to establish a certain familiarity. Very often they beset tender girls, to whom they manifest themselves as handsome gallants, hot young amorosos, who pursue them with obscene suggestions, whispering in their ears the most indecent words at unguarded moments.*

"Not long since," says Coleti, "a country wench, accompanied by her father, came to consult me. She complained that she was persecuted by an incubus who had appeared to her more than once, but curiously enough under the form of a most unlovely and evil-favoured old cullion. When the girl ran away in fright she found that he was hard at her heels. He often used, at suppertime, to carry off the slice of bread which had been cut for her, leaving the victuals

of the others untouched. A thousand petty persecutions followed, until the constant annoyance became intolerable. Accordingly, well-nigh in despair, they applied to me for some means of relief. I took the necessary measures, and by a strong exorcism conjured the incubus to cease his molestations. This happy result was secured, and the damsel forthwith entirely relieved from such mysterious importunities."

In somewhat the same way an incubus seemed to have attached himself to Maggie, a farmer's daughter, a girl about twenty years old, whose family lived near the hamlet of Derrygonelly, County Fermanagh. The case was investigated by Professor Barrett, the Rev. Maxwell Close, and Mr. Thomas Plunkett, of Enniskillen. Curiously enough the lutin was banished without any great trouble or effort (Proceedings of the Society for Psychical Research, *August*, 1911 ; *a paper by Professor Barrett, pp.* 377–395).

Girolamo Menghi, the famous Capuchin demonologist, relates the following incidents which actually passed under his own observation. In 1579 there was living at Bologna a rich merchant whose house was impested by a mischievous lutin. For some weeks the family attributed the noises and extraordinary disorders to the naughty pranks of the children or pageboys, but it soon became evident that they could not be contrived by any natural means. That they might avoid silly gossip and the laughter of neighbours, matters were concealed as long as possible, but in time the nuisance became too plaguy to be borne, and the master of the house had resource to experienced theologians and exorcists, who, however, proved powerless to relieve the situation. The *lutin had fondly attached himself to one of the serving-maids, whom he seemed to follow whithersoever she went. He even espoused her cause, and after she had been scolded for some negligence by her mistress the lady was slapped and pinched by him, her headdress torn, and cold water thrown upon her as she lay in bed. When the girl herself began to take measures to rid herself of him he got angry, and suddenly stripped her of her clothes, then, as she wept and screamed aloud, he incontinently dressed her again in the same garments and tried to console her. However, Fra Girolamo, owing to his vast knowledge of these hauntings, was able to expel the lutin, who, after having vented his rage in angry words to the young girl and in threats against her master, abandoned the scene and ceased his perse-cution.*

Very similar incidents took place during the following year in the same city at the house of another merchant, where the incubus was attracted by a young lass of fifteen, who had recently entered the family to be trained in domestic duties. But the lutin raised such serious dis-turbances, breaking ewers of waters and bottles of wine, spoiling food, moving the heaviest articles of furniture from place to place with incredible swiftness, and doing, in fine, considerable damage, that it was found impossible by the good man of the house to retain the girl in his service. She was accordingly sent away, and at her departure peace was restored. No doubt she was strongly mediumistic, for this account may be closely paralleled with the manifestations that took place in Turin, at No. 6 Via Bava, and which were investigated by Professor Lombroso in 1900. Here bottles of wine fell over of their own accord and were smashed to pieces. This was seen on many occasions by independent witnesses. The furniture, platters, scaldini, pots and pans, were hurled in all directions, and the place became a regular Donnybrook Fair. So great was the tumult that the police took charge, but proved utterly unable to cope with the invisible activities. " The manifestations ceased when a boy employed in the shop was dismissed. It was conclusively proved that he could not have manipulated the phenomena, which often occurred when he was absent, but no doubt he possessed unusual mediumistic faculties which gave the power an opportunity to concentrate itself and cause the disturbance."

Certainly the two serving-girls at Bologna, of whom Menghi tells us, were exceptionally mediumistic, although quite unconscious of their powers, and this was probably also the case with the Nun at Pavia ; the Carthusian ; Signora Hieronyma ; and others of whom Sinistrari gives us his first-hand account.

The propositions which Sinistrari advances in his Demoniality *are, it is worth remarking, closely akin to the theories of the celebrated Paracelsus* (1493–1541), *who was initiated into all the mysteries of alchemy by Joannes Trithemius, the Benedictine Abbot of Sponheim,* Germanae gloria gentis.

These theories, to wit, that the elements are peopled by spiritual beings, or, rather, by beings not purely spiritual, since in certain circumstances it was supposed that they could perform the peculiarly human act of coition, had immense influence during the sixteenth, seventeenth, and eighteenth centuries. Popular rumour declared that this was the belief of the theosophical Rosicrucians, and pre-

sently a whole literature, both serious and fanciful, grew up around the subject. One work in particular may be cited. In 1670 the abbé Montfaucon de Villars published his Le Comte de Gabalis, ou Entretiens sur les sciences secrètes, *a book which enjoyed the most extraordinary success, which ran into edition after edition, was translated and retranslated, and has left a lasting mark upon our own literature. The machinery of* The Rape of the Lock *was inspired by de Villars, and the poet, in his dedication to Mrs. Arabella Fermor, playfully says : "* The Rosicrucians *are a People I must bring you acquainted with. The best Account I know of them is in a French Book called* Le Comte de Gabalis, *which both in its Title and Size is so like a Novel, that many of the Fair Sex have read it for one by Mistake. According to these Gentlemen the four Elements are inhabited by Spirits, which they call* Sylphs, Gnomes, Nymphs, *and* Salamanders. The Gnomes, *or Dæmons of Earth, delight in Mischief : but the* Sylphs, *whose Habitation is Air, are the best-conditioned Creatures imaginable. For they say, any Mortals may enjoy the most intimate Familiarities with these gentle Spirits, upon a Condition very easy to all true* Adepts, *an inviolate Preservation of Chastity."*

Actually very little is recorded concerning the abbé de Villars. We know that he met a tragic fate, for he was found assassinated in the country not far from Lyons ; slain by the sylphs, Voltaire mockingly said, since he had dared to reveal their secrets to the world. His contemporaries considered Le Comte de Gabalis *an elegant trifle ; some writers since have discerned a serious mean-*

ing in this little book. They suggest that by his extravagances the author wished to lead men on the rebound towards sheer rationalism; others again, and the truth seems to lie here, have been shrewd enough to divine that beneath his fantasies and imagery there lies a vein of serious speculation.

Le Comte de Gabalis *was followed by numberless imitations. Thus we have* l'Histoire des imaginations extravagantes de M. Oufle *by the abbé Bordelon, who draws upon Cornelius Agrippa, Delrio, Bodin, Le Loyer, and many other occult writers. Cabalistic romances were the rage, but it is hardly necessary nor possible here to consider so vast a library which rosily faded away into such pretty works as* Les Ondins, L'Amant Salamandre, *and* Le Sylphe Amoureux.

A curious volume is " Sub-Mundanes ; or, The Elementaries of the Cabula : *Being The History of Spirits Reprinted from the Text of the Abbe de Villars,* Physio-Astro-Mystic, *Wherein is asserted that there are in existance* [sic] *on earth rational creatures besides man. With an illustrative Appendix from the Work* ' Demoniality ' *or* ' Incubi and Succubi ' *by the Rev. Father Sinistrari, of Ameno.* ' Honi soit qui mal y pense.' *Privately Printed only for Subscribers.* Bath 1886." *A second title is :* " The Count of Gabalis ; or, The Extravagant Mysteries of the Cabalists Exposed, In Five Pleasant Discourses On the Secret Sciences." *As an appendix are given in Latin two passages from Sinistrari : No.* 30; *and No.* 3 *of the* Probatio. *It is difficult to see why the book should have been printed at all. It has no notes, no introduction, and is a silly, feckless, impotent sort of thing.*

Sinistrari's Demoniality, *the Latin text with a French translation,* De La Démonialité et des Animaux Incubes et Succubes, *was first published (Paris, 8vo, 1875) by the celebrated bibliophile Isidore Liseux, who issued it from his house, 2 Rue Bonaparte. Liseux had discovered the manuscript in London in 1872, and gives the following account of its provenance. He relates how he used to frequent the shop of a certain Mr. Allen, " a venerable old gentleman, whose place of business was in the Euston Road, close to the gate of Regent's Park." Mr. Allen seems to have sold his stock according to size, folios and quartos at two or three shillings apiece ; octavos at one shilling ; and duodecimos at sixpence. He methodically bought in his volumes at the book auctions, and among these lots rare volumes not unseldom chanced to come his way for a handful of coppers. On one occasion, from the 6 to the 16 December, 1871, Sotheby was selling the library of Seymour Kirkup, an English collector, who some months before had died in Florence, and Mr. Allen then acquired a number of books and manuscripts which had been neglected by Quaritch, Sotheran, Pickering, and the rest. A little while after, Liseux, who happened to be in the shop, turned over various specimens of these late Italian codices. The title of one was* De Uenenis ; *of another* De Uiperis ; *of a third* De Dæmonialitate et Incubis, et Succubis. *All three were separate, and by several authors. " Poisons, adders, demons," he cries, " what a collection of horrors ! Yet, were it but for civility's sake, I was bound to buy something." He decided to choose the last, and for sixpence he became the possessor of Sinistrari's work. In 1879 he was advertis-*

ing for sale " the original manuscript of Demoniality,"
*for which he asked forty pounds, not a bad return on the
humble tester he had originally laid out in Mr. Allen's
shop.*

*The manuscript in Sotheby's sale catalogue is listed as
follows :—*

> *No.* 145. AMENO (R. P. *Ludovicus Maria*
> [Cotta] *de*). De Dæmonialitate, et Incubis, et
> Succubis, *Manuscript.*
>
> *Sæc. XVII–XVIII.*

*This manuscript, written on strong paper of the seven-
teenth century, bound in Italian parchment, and beutifully
preserved, has eighty-six pages of text. The title and first
page are in the author's hand, that of an old man. The
remainder is in very clear, and probably professional, calli-
graphy, made under Sinistrari's direction, as is obvious
from the side notes and corrections in his quavering script,
which occur throughout the whole work. It was, no doubt,
taken down from his dictation, and thus is certainly the
original manuscript.*

*Liseux, apparently, found it far from easy to trace
Sinistrari, although, in truth, this should not have been a
very difficult task. It is to be feared that he set about it in
rather an unintelligent way. He applied to the librarian
of St. Sulpice, and at the Capuchins, whose house was
then in the Rue de la Santé. But Sinistrari's works could
not be found in either of these convents. Indeed, it was a
bookseller at Milan who was first able to furnish Liseux
with tractates by Sinistrari, and thus enable him to establish the identity of the famous theologian. Liseux seems
to have sent a copy of* De La Démonialité, *8vo, 1875,*

to the Rev. Father Provincial of the Capuchins, and he received in reply the following letter, which is certainly worth reprinting :—

P..., *Friday* (8 *October* 1875).

+

Pax

MONS. ISIDORE LISEUX,

Paris.

I have gone through the work you sent me yesterday, and have, indeed, been satisfied with the edition ; the time has not yet arrived for me to give my opinion on the value of the work itself. Here you would have met with no other works of the Rev. Father Sinistrari of Ameno than his book : Practica criminalis Minorum ; De Delictis et Pœnis *is to be found, I believe, in another of our convents ; but you would have been given a most welcome reception.*

I believe that Des Grieux can hardly have resided in the present St. Sulpice, which dates but from the year 1816. . . . *So far as a superficial glance has enabled me to ascertain, there are some other mistakes ; but, altogether, the work is a good one, and you may accept of the congratulations of*

Your very little servant,

F. A...

o.m.c.

m.p.

Convent of Capuchins, rue....

This is a candid criticism of Sinistrari's work.

Myself, I have endeavoured to state the case in support of his thesis as impartially as possible. Nobody is bound

*to accept his hypothesis ; at the same time it is both theo-
logically and philosophically defensible. There is nothing
in his treatise that is not perfectly consonant with the
soundest orthodoxy, and it is far better to believe too much
than too little. Perhaps there are some superficial errors,
but nothing of moment. In fact the theory of Father Sinistrari offers an explanation of many cases of haunting
which otherwise it were impossible to place or understand.
Not that the explanation could cover more than a limited
number of these extraordinary phenomena. So universal
and so varied are they that we cannot reasonably hope to
find a common factor to them all. Indeed, it were not
temerarious to say we know such not to be the case. However, until it has been theologically disproved, I, for one, am
willing to accept, with certain minor reservations, the
thesis that the octogenarian Sinistrari, rich in wisdom and
experience, laid down in his* Dæmoniality *more than two
hundred years ago.*

MONTAGUE SUMMERS.

In Festo vij Dolorum B.M.V. in Quadragesima,
1927.

DEMONIALITY

THE first author who, so far as I know, uses the word *Demoniality* is Juan Caramuel, in his *Fundamental Theology*, and before him I can find no one who distinguishes that crime from *Bestiality*. Indeed, all Moral Theologians, following S. Thomas (II. 2, quest. 154), include, under the specific title of *Bestiality*, " *every kind of carnal intercourse with any thing whatsoever of a different species* " : such are the words used by S. Thomas. Cajetan, for instance, in his commentary on that Question, classes intercourse with the Demon under the description of Bestiality ; so does Silvester, *de Luxuria ;* Bonacina, *de Matrimonio*, quest. 4; and others.

2. However, it is clear that in the above passage S. Thomas did not allude to intercourse with the Demon. And as shall be demonstrated further on, that intercourse cannot be included in the particular and peculiar species *Bestiality ;* and, in order to make that sentence of the holy Doctor tally with truth, it must be admitted that when saying of unnatural sin, " *that committed through intercourse with a thing of different species, it takes the name of Bestiality*," S. Thomas, by *a thing of different species*, means a living animal, of another species than man : for he could not here use the word *thing* in its most general sense, to mean indiscriminately an animate or inanimate being. In fact, if a man should fornicate with a dead body, he would have to do with a thing

of a species quite different from his own (especially according to the Thomists, who deny the form of human corporeity in a corpse) ; similarly if he were to have connexion with a dead animal : yet, such copulation would not be bestiality, but pollution. What therefore S. Thomas intended here to specify so exactly is carnal intercourse with a living thing of a species different from man, that is to say, with an animal, and he assuredly intends no reference to intercourse with the Demon.

3. Therefore, connexion with the Demon, whether Incubus or Succubus (which is, properly speaking, *Demoniality*), differs in kind from Bestiality, and does not in conjunction with it form one particular species, as Cajetan wrongly maintains ; for, whatever may have been said to the contrary by some early authorities, and later by Caramuel in his *Fundamental Theology*, by Vincenzo Filliucci, and others, unnatural sins differ from each other most distinctly. Such at least is the general doctrine, and the contrary opinion has been condemned by Alexander VII. (No. XXIV. of the condemned propositions) : first, because each of those sins carries with itself its peculiar and distinct turpitude, opposed to chastity and to human procreation ; secondly, because the commission thereof entails each time the sacrifice of some good by reason of the nature attached to the institution of the venereal act, the normal end of which is human generation ; lastly, because each has a different motive, which in itself is sufficient to bring about, in divers and several

ways, the deprivation of the same good, as has been clearly shown by Filliucci, Crespinus, and Caramuel.

4. It follows that Demoniality differs in kind from Bestiality, for each has its peculiar and distinct turpitude, opposed to chastity and human procreation. Bestiality is connexion with a living beast, endowed with its own proper senses and impulses ; Demoniality, on the contrary, is copulation with a corpse (in accordance at least with the general opinion which shall be considered hereafter), a senseless and motionless corpse which is but accidentally moved through the power of the Demon. Now, if fornication with the dead body of a man, or a woman, or a beast differ in kind from Sodomy and Bestiality, there is the same difference with regard to *Demoniality*, which, according to the general opinion, is the intercourse of man with a dead body accidentally endued with motion.

5. Another proof follows : in sins against nature, the unnatural semination (which cannot be regularly followed by procreation) is a genus ; but the object of such semination is the difference which marks the species under the genus. Thus, whether semination takes place on the ground, or on an inanimate body, it is pollution ; if with a male *in uase præpostero*, it is Sodomy (*Sodomia perfecta*) ; with a beast, Bestiality : crimes which unquestionably all differ from each other in species, just as the ground, the corpse, the man and the beast, passive objects of such emission of semen, differ in species from each

other. But the difference between the Demon and the beast is not only specific, it is more than specific : the nature of the one is corporeal, of the other incorporeal, which makes a generic difference. Whence it follows that several emissions of semen practised on different objects differ in species from each other : and that is, according to the intention of the act.

6. It is also a common doctrine with Moralists, established by the Council of Trent, session 14, and approved by S. Thomas, Gabriel Vasquez, Enrique Henriquez, Bartholomew Medina, and other theologians, that in confession it suffices to state the circumstances which alter the species of sins. If therefore Demoniality and Bestiality belonged to the very same particular species, it would be enough that, each time he has fornicated with the Demon, the penitent should say to his confessor : *I have been guilty of the sin of Bestiality*. But that is not the case : therefore those two sins do not both belong to the very same particular species.

7. It may be urged that if the circumstances of copulation with the Demon should be revealed to the confessor, it is on account of the offence against Religion, an offence which comes either from the worship rendered to the Demon, or from the homage or prayers offered up to him, or from the compact of fellowship entered into with him (*S. Thomas*, II. 2, Quest. 90, art. 2, and Quest. 95, art. 4). But, as will be seen hereafter, there are Incubi and Succubi to whom none of the foregoing applies, and yet there is carnal connexion. There is consequently,

in that special case, no element of irreligion, no other character than of plain and simple fornication; and, if it were the same species as Bestiality, it would have to be confessed by clearly stating : *I have been guilty of the sin of Bestiality;* which is not the case.

8. Besides, it is acknowledged by all Moral Theologians that carnal connexion with the Devil, or a familiar, is much more heinous than the same act committed with any beast whatsoever. Now, in the same particular and peculiar species of sins, one sin is not more heinous than another; all are equally grave : it is the same whether connexion is had with a bitch, an ass, or a mare ; whence it follows that if *Demoniality* is more heinous than Bestiality, those two acts are not of the same species. And let it not be argued, with Cajetan (II. 2, Quest. 154, art. 2, towards the end of III.), that *Demoniality* is always more heinous on account of the offence to religion from the worship rendered to the Demon or the compact of fellowship entered into with him: since it has been shown above, that these circumstances do not always occur in the connexion of man with Incubi and Succubi ; moreover, if in the genus of unnatural sin *Demoniality* is more grievous than Bestiality, the offence to Religion is quite foreign to that aggravation, and accidental, since it is foreign to that genus itself.

9. Therefore, having laid down the specific difference between *Demoniality* and Bestiality, so that the gravity thereof may be duly appreciated in view

of the penalty to be inflicted (and that is our most essential object), we must needs inquire in how many different ways the sin of *Demoniality* may be committed. There is no lack of people who, mightily proud of their small stock of knowledge, venture to deny what has been written by the gravest authors and what is, moreover, testified by every day experience : namely, that the Demon, whether Incubus or Succubus, unites carnally not only with men and women, but also with beasts. They allege that it all proceeds from the human imagination troubled by the craft of the Demon, and that it is nothing but phantasmagoria, glamour, and diabolical spells. The like happens, they say, to Witches who, under the influence of an illusion brought on by the Demon, imagine that they attend the nightly sports, dances, revels and sabbats, and there have carnal intercourse with the Demon, though in reality they are not bodily transferred to those places nor do they take any part in these abominations. But the reality and the truth of all this have been explicitly laid down by Episcopal Capitularies, by the Council of Ancyra, by the Roman synods under Pope S. Damasus I. These are cited by Lorinus of Avignon.

10. Of course, there is no question that sometimes young women, deceived by the Demon, imagine they are actually taking part, in their flesh and blood, in the sabbats of Witches, and all this is merest fantasy. Thus, in a dream, one sometimes fancies that one is sleeping with someone else, and there is an emission of semen, yet that connexion is

wholly unreal and imaginary, and often brought about by a diabolical illusion : and here the above-mentioned Episcopal Capitularies and Councils are perfectly right. But this is not always the case ; on the contrary, it more often happens that Witches are bodily present at sabbats and have an actual carnal and corporeal connexion with the Demon, and that likewise Wizards copulate with the Succubus or female Demon. Such is the opinion of Theologians as well as of jurists, many of whose names will be found at length in the *Compendium Maleficarum*, or *Chronicle of Witches*, by Fra Francesco Maria Guazzo. It is maintained by Grilland, Remy, S. Peter Damian, Silvester, Alfonso à Castro, Cajetan, Père Pierre Crespet, Bartolomeo Spina, Giovanni Lorenzo Anania. This doctrine is also therein confirmed by eighteen actual instances adduced from the recitals of learned and truthful men whose testimony is beyond suspicion, and which prove that Wizards and Witches are indeed bodily present at sabbats and most shamefully copulate with Demons, Incubi or Succubi. And, after all, to settle the question, we have the authority of S. Augustine, who, speaking of carnal intercourse between men and the Demon, expresses himself as follows, book xvth, chap. 23rd, of the *City of God : " It is widely credited, and such belief is confirmed by the direct or indirect testimony of thoroughly trustworthy people, that Sylvans and Fauns, commonly called Incubi, have frequently molested women, sought and obtained from them coition. There are even Demons, whom the Gauls call Duses or Boggarts, who very regularly indulge in those unclean practices : the fact is testified by so many and such weighty authorities, that it were impudent to doubt it."* Such are the very words of S. Augustine.

11. Now, several authors assert, and it is confirmed by numerous experiments, that the Demon has two ways of copulating carnally with men or women : the one which he uses with Witches or Wizards, the other with men or women who know nothing of witchcraft.

12. In the first case, the Demon does not copulate with Witches or Wizards until after a solemn profession, in virtue of which such wretched creatures yield themselves up to him. According to several authors who have related the judicial admissions of Witches when on the rack, and whose recitals have been collected by Francesco Maria Guazzo, *Compendium Maleficarum*, book 1, chap. 7, that profession consists of eleven ceremonials :

13. Firstly, the Novices have to conclude with the Demon, or with some other Wizard or Magician acting in the Demon's place, an express compact by which, in the presence of witnesses, they enlist in the Demon's service, he giving them in exchange his promise that they shall enjoy honours, riches and carnal pleasures. Guazzo ; *loc. cit.*

14. Secondly, they abjure the Catholic Faith, withdraw from their obedience to God, renounce Christ and the protection of the most Blessed Virgin Mary, and all the Sacraments of the Church. Guazzo; *loc. cit.*

15. Thirdly, they cast away the Crown, or Rosary

of the most Blessed Virgin Mary, the girdle of S. Francis, or the Cincture of S. Augustine, or the Scapular of the Carmelites, should they belong to one of those Orders; the Cross, the Medals, the *Agnus Dei*, whatever other holy or consecrated object may have been about their person, and trample them under foot. Guazzo, *loc. cit.*; Grilland, passim.

16. Fourthly, into the hands of the Devil they vow obedience and subjection; they pay him homage and vassalage, laying their fingers on some foul black book. They bind themselves never to return to the faith of Christ, to observe none of the divine precepts, to do no good work, but to obey the Demon alone and to attend diligently the nightly conventicles. Guazzo; *loc. cit.*

17. Fifthly, they promise to strive with all their power, and to devote their utmost zeal and care to the enlistment of other males and females in the service of the Demon. Guazzo; *loc. cit.*

18. Sixthly, the Devil administers to them a certain sacrilegious baptism, and after abjuring their Christian Godfathers and Godmothers of the Baptism of Christ and Confirmation, they have assigned to them a new Godfather and a new Godmother, who are to instruct them in the arts of witchcraft; they drop their former name and exchange it for another, more frequently a scurrilous and absurd nickname. Guazzo; *loc. cit.*

19. Seventhly, they cut off a part of their own garments, and tender it as a token of homage to the

Devil, who takes it away and retains it. Guazzo ; *loc. cit.*

20. Eighthly, the Devil draws on the ground a circle wherein stand the Novices, Witches and Wizards, and there they confirm by horrid oaths all their aforesaid promises. Guazzo ; *loc. cit.*

21. Ninthly, they request the Devil to strike them out of the book of Christ, and to inscribe them in his own book. Then is brought forth that foul black book on which, as has been explained above, they laid hands when doing homage, and they are inscribed therein with the Devil's claw. Guazzo ; *loc. cit.*

22. Tenthly, they promise the Devil sacrifices and offerings at stated times : once a fortnight or at least each month, the slaughter of some child, or a murderous act of sorcery, and week by week other vile misdeeds to the bitter hurt of mankind, such as hailstorms, tempests, fires, rinderpest, the destruction of sheep and kine, etc. Guazzo ; *loc. cit.*

23. Eleventhly, the Demon imprints on them some mark, especially on those whose constancy he suspects. That mark, moreover, is not always of the same shape or figure : sometimes it is the likeness of a hare, sometimes a toad's foot, sometimes a spider, a puppy, a dormouse. It is imprinted on the most hidden parts of the body : with men, under the eye-lids, or it may be under the armpits, or on the lips, on the shoulder, the fundament, or somewhere else ; with women, it is usually on the breasts or the privy parts. Now, the stamp which imprints

those marks is none other but the Devil's claw. When all these rites have been performed in accordance with the instructions of the mystagogues who initiate the novices, these then promise never to worship the Blessed Sacrament; to insult all Saints and especially the most Holy Mother of God ; to trample under foot and defile Holy Images, the Cross, and the Relics of Saints ; never to use the sacraments or sacramentals ; never to make a good confession to the priest, but to keep always hidden from him their intercourse with the Demon. The Demon, in exchange, engages to give them always prompt assistance ; to fulfil their desires in this world and to make them happy after their death. The solemn profession being thus made, each has assigned to himself a Devil called *Magistellus* or Little Master, with whom he retires aside for carnal satisfaction ; the said Devil assuming the shape of a woman if the initiated person be a man, the shape of a man, sometimes of a satyr, sometimes of a buck-goat, if it be a woman who has been received a witch. Guazzo ; *loc. cit.*

24. If we seek to learn from these Authorities how it is possible that the Demon, who has no body, yet can perform actual coitus with man or woman, they unanimously answer that the Demon assumes the corpse of another human being, male or female as the case may be, or that, from the mixture of other materials, he shapes for himself a body endowed with motion, by means of which body he copulates with the human being ; and they add that

when women are desirous of becoming pregnant by
the Demon (which occurs only with the consent and
at the express wish of the said women), the Demon is
transformed into a Succubus, and during the act of
coition with some man receives therefrom human
semen ; or else he procures pollution from a man
during his sleep, and then he preserves the spilt
semen at its natural heat, conserving it with the
vital essence. This, when he has connexion with
the woman, he introduces into her womb, whence
follows impregnation. Such is the teaching of
Guazzo, book 1, ch. 12, and he proves it by a
number of quotations and instances taken from many
learned Doctors.

25. At other times also the Demon, whether Incubus or Succubus, copulates with men or women
from whom, however, he receives none of the
sacrifices, homage or offerings which he is wont to
exact from Wizards or Witches, as aforesaid. He is
then but a passionate lover, having only one desire ;
the carnal possession of those whom his lust craves.
Of this there are numerous instances to be found in
authors of no small repute, amongst whom we read
of the case of Menippus Lycius, who long cohabited
with a woman, and when she had served him sexually
many times and oft, so doted on her that she persuaded him to marry her ; but a certain philosopher,
who happened to be present at the wedding ban-
quet, having guessed what the woman was, told
Menippus that he had to deal with a *Compusa*, that
is a Succubus ; whereupon the bride vanished

shrieking and wailing bitterly. Such is the narrative related by Cœlius Rhodiginus, *Antiquitatum*, book xxix., ch. 5. Hector Boece (*Scotorum Historiæ*, book viii.), also relates the adventure of a young Scotchman, who, during many months, although the doors and windows of his chamber were ever fast shut, was visited in his bed-room by a Succubus of the most enchanting beauty; she resorted to every blandishment, caresses, kisses, embraces, entreaties, to prevail upon him to fornicate with her : but she could not succeed with the chaste young man.

26. We read likewise of numerous women incited to coition by an Incubus, and who, though reluctant at first of yielding to him, are soon moved by his prayers, tears, and endearments ; for he is a desperate lover and must not be denied. And although this comes sometimes of the craft of some Wizard who avails himself of the agency of the Demon, yet the Demon not infrequently acts thus on his own account, as Guazzo informs us, *Compendium Maleficarum*, III. 8 ; and this happens not only with women, but also with mares ; for if they readily comply with his desire, he pets them, and plaits their manes in elaborate and inextricably reticulated tresses ; but if they resist, he ill-treats and strikes them, infects them with the glanders and lampass, and may finally kill them, as is shown by daily experience.

27. It is a most marvellous and well nigh incomprehensible fact that the Incubi whom the Italians call *Folletti*, the Spaniards *Duendes*, the French

Follets, do not obey the Exorcists, evince no dread of exorcisms, and show no reverence for holy things, at the approach of which seemingly they are not overawed. Now they are very different in this respect from the Demons who vex those whom they possess ; for, however obstinate those evil Spirits may be, however resistant to the injunctions of the Exorcist who bids them leave the body they possess, yet, at the mere utterance of the Most Holy Names of Jesus or Mary, or the recitation of some verses of Scripture, at the imposition of Relics, especially of the Wood of the Most Holy Cross, or at the sight of pictures and statues of the Saints, they roar fearfully from the mouth of the possessed person, they gnash, shake, quiver, and display fright and terror. But the Folletti show none of those signs, and only desist their vexations after a very long space of time. Of this I was an eye-witness, and I shall relate a story which verily passes human belief : but I take God to witness that I tell the actual truth, corroborated by the testimony of many reputable persons.

28. About twenty-five years ago, when I was lecturer on Sacred Theology in the convent of the Holy Cross, in Pavia, there was living in that city a married woman of unimpeachable morality, and who was most highly spoken of by all such as knew her, especially by the Friars. Her name was Hieronyma, and she lived in the parish of S. Michael. One day, this woman had kneaded bread at home and given it out to bake. The cook-shop man brought her back her loaves when baked, and

with them a large cake of a peculiar shape, made of butter and Venetian paste, as is usual for manchets to be made in that city. She declined to take it in, saying she had not kneaded any thing of the kind. "But," said the cook, "I had no other bread save yours to bake to-day, therefore this cake also must have come from your house; you have, perhaps, forgotten." The good wife allowed herself to be persuaded, and partook of the cake with her husband, her little girl who was three years old, and the maid servant. The next night, whilst in bed with her husband, and both were fast asleep, she suddenly woke up at the sound of a very small voice, something like a shrill hissing, whispering in her ears, yet with great distinctness, and inquiring whether "the cake had been to her taste?" The good woman, thoroughly frightened, began to guard herself with the sign of the cross and repeatedly called upon the Names of Jesus and Mary. "Be not afraid," said the voice, "I mean you no harm; quite the reverse: I am prepared to do anything to please you; I am captivated by your beauty, and desire nothing more than to enjoy your sweet embraces." Whereupon she felt somebody kissing her cheeks, so lightly, so softly, that she might have fancied being stroked by the finest feather-down. She resisted without giving any answer, confidently repeating over and over again the Names of Jesus and Mary, and crossing herself most devoutly. The tempter kept on thus for nearly half an hour, when he withdrew.

The next morning the dame sought her confessor, a discreet and learned man, who confirmed and encouraged her in her faith, exhorting her to maintain her stout resistance and to provide herself with some holy Relics. On the ensuing nights she was sore tempted with the same amorous words and loving kisses, and she showed the same constancy in repulsing them. Utterly weary, however, of such painful and persistent molestations, upon the advice of her confessor and other reverend men, she had herself exorcised by experienced Exorcists, in order to ascertain whether perchance she was not actually possessed. Having found in her no trace of the evil Spirit, they blessed the house, the bedroom, the bed, and strictly commanded the Incubus to cease his annoyance. But all was in vain ; he kept on worse than before, pretending to be love-sick, weeping and moaning in order to melt the heart of the lady, who however, by the grace of God, remained unconquered. The Incubus then went another way to work : he showed himself in the shape of a lad or little man of great beauty, with crisped golden locks, a flaxen beard that shone like fine gold, sea-green eyes calling to mind the flax-flower, and arrayed in a comely Spanish dress. Besides he appeared to her even when she was in company, billing and cooing gently after the fashion of lovers, kissing his hand to her, and continually endeavouring by such means to obtain her embraces. She alone saw and heard him : to everybody else he was invisible.

This good lady kept persevering in her disdain with admirable constancy until, at last, after some months of courting, the Incubus, angered at her insensibility, had recourse to a new kind of persecution. First, he took away from her a silver cross filled with sacred Relics, and a holy wax or papal Agnus Dei of the blessed Pontiff Pius V., which she always carried on her person; then, although it could not be found that the locks had been tampered with or opened, he purloined her rings and other gold and silver ornaments and jewelry from the casket wherein they were stored. Next, he began to strike her cruelly, and after each beating, livid bruises and discolorations were to be seen on her face, her arms and other parts of her body, which lasted a day or two, then suddenly disappeared, the reverse of natural bruises which heal slowly and by degrees. Sometimes, too, while she was nursing her little girl, he would snatch the child away from her breast and lay it upon the roof, on the edge of the gutter, or hide it, but without ever harming it. Sometimes he would upset all the furniture, or smash to pieces saucepans, plates, and other earthenware utensils which, in a twink, he restored incontinently to their former whole state. One night whilst she was lying by her husband's side, the Incubus, appearing in his customary shape, vehemently urged his desires, which she steadfastly resisted as usual. He thereupon withdrew in a rage, and shortly after came back with a large load of those flag stones which the Genoese, and the inhabitants of Liguria in general, use for roofing their houses. With those stones he built around the bed a wall so high that it reached the tester, and the couple were unable to leave their bed without using a ladder. This wall, however, was built up unmortared, without lime; and when pulled down, the flags were laid by in a corner where, during two days, they were seen of many who came to look at them; they then disappeared.

On S. Stephen's day, the husband had asked some military friends to dinner, and, to do fitting honour to his guests, provided a substantial repast. Whilst they were, as customary, washing their hands before taking their places, suddenly the table, just ready laid, vanished clean away from the dining-room; all the dishes, saucepans, colanders, kettles, plates and crockery in the kitchen vanished likewise, as well as the jacks, jugs, bottles, beakers, and glasses. The guests, eight in number, stood, surprised and confounded, in strange amaze. Amongst them, as it chanced, was a Spanish Captain of infantry, who, addressing the company, said boldly : " Do not be alarmed, it is but a trick : the table is certainly still where it was, and I shall soon find it by feeling for it." With these words, he paced round the room holding his arms wide outstretched, and endeavouring to lay hold of the table ; but when, after much groping and walking to and fro, it was apparent that his efforts were useless, since he continually grasped nought but thin air, he was well laughed at by his friends ; and it being already high time and past for having dinner, each guest took up his cloak and was about to return home. They had already reached the street-door with their host, the husband, who, out of politeness, was attending them, when they heard a great crash in the dining-room. Astonished beyond measure, they paused awhile wondering what the cause of such a noise might be, and lo! the servant ran up hastily to announce that the kitchen was stocked with new vessels filled with food, and that the table was standing again in its former place. Having gone back to the dining-room, they were dumbfounded to see the table indeed was laid, with napery, napkins, salt-cellars, silver cruets, castors, trenchers and trays that did not belong to the house, and groaning with rich meats, pasties, pullets and puddings, which certainly had not been cooked there. On a large sideboard, too, were arrayed in perfect order crystal, silver, and gold cups, with all manner of flagons, decanters and lusty bowls filled with rare foreign wines, from the Isle of Crete, Campania, the Canaries, and the Rhine. In the kitchen there was also an abundant variety of viands, fish and game, in saucepans and dishes that had never been seen there before. At first, some of the guests much hesitated whether they should partake of that food ; however, encouraged by others, they sat down, and soon ate heartily, for the dishes proved to be of exquisite flavour. Immediately afterwards, when dinner was done, as they were sitting before a good winter fire, everything vanished away, the dishes, the very orts and crumbs, and in their stead reappeared the table of the house, laid with a cloth, and thereupon the victuals which had been previously cooked; but, for a wonder, all the guests were fully satisfied, so that no one could think of supper after such a magnificent dinner. A clear proof this that the substituted viands were real and nowise fictitious.

This kind of persecution had been going on for some months, when the lady betook herself to the Blessed Bernardine of Feltre, whose body is venerated in the Church of S. James, a short distance from the walls of the city. She made a vow to him that she would wear, during a whole twelve-month, a sad-coloured frock, girt about her waist with a cord, such as is worn by the Friars Minor, the Order of which Blessed Bernardine was a member. This she vowed, in the hope that, through his intercession, she might at last be rid of the persecution of the Incubus. And accordingly, on the 28 September, the vigil of the Dedication of the Archangel S. Michael, and the festival of the Blessed Bernardine, she donned the votive habit. The next morning, which was Michaelmas Day, the afflicted woman repaired to the church of S. Michael, her own parish, already mentioned. It was now about ten o'clock, a time when crowds of people were going to mass. She had no sooner set foot on the threshold of the church, than her clothes and ornaments fell to the ground, and disappeared in a gust of wind, leaving her mother naked. There happened, fortunately, to be among the crowd two cavaliers of mature age, who, seeing what had taken place, very decently hastened to divest themselves of their cloaks with which they concealed, as well as they could, the woman's nudity, and having put her into a close coach, accompanied her home. The clothes and trinkets carried off by the Incubus were not restored by him before six months had elapsed.

I might not impertinently relate many other most amazing tricks and naughty japeries which that Incubus played on her, were it not wearisome. Suffice it to say that, for a number of years, he persevered in his temptation of her, but that, finding at last he was losing his pains, he desisted from his vexatious and wanton importunities.

29. In the above case, as well as in others that may be occasionally heard or read of, the Incubus attempts no act against Religion ; he merely assails chastity. Consequently, consent is not a sin through ungodliness, but merely through incontinence.

30. Now, it is undoubted by Theologians and philosophers that carnal intercourse between mankind and the Demon sometimes gives birth to human beings ; and that is how Antichrist is to be born, according to some Doctors, for example, Bellarmine, Suarez, and Thomas Malvenda. They further observe that, from a natural cause, the children thus begotten by Incubi are tall, very hardy and bloodily bold, arrogant beyond words, and desperately wicked. Thus writes Malvenda ; as for the cause, he gives it from Franciscus Valesius :

" What Incubi introduce into the womb, is not any ordinary human semen in normal quantity, but abundant, very thick, very warm, rich in spirits and free from serosity. This, moreover, is an easy thing for them, since they merely have to choose ardent, robust men, whose semen is naturally very copious, and with whom the Succubus has connexion, and then women of a like constitution, with whom the Incubus copulates, taking care that both shall enjoy a more than normal orgasm, for the more abundant is the semen the greater the venereal excitement." Those are the words of Valesius, confirmed by Malvenda who shows, from the testimony of various classical Authors, that such conjunctions gave birth to : Romulus and Remus, according to *Livy* and *Plutarch ;* Servius-Tullius, the sixth king of Rome, according to *Dionysius of Halicarnassus* and *Pliny the Elder ;* Plato the Philosopher, according to *Diogenes Laertius* and *Saint Jerome ;* Alexander the Great, according to *Plutarch* and *Quintus Curtius ;* Seleucus, king of Syria, according to *Justin* and *Appian ;* Scipio Africanus the Elder, according to *Livy ;* the emperor Cæsar Augustus, according to *Suetonius ;* Aristomenes the Messenian, an illustrious Greek commander, according to *Strabo* and *Pausanias ;* as also Merlin or Melchin the Englishman, born from an Incubus and a nun, the daughter of Charlemagne ; Hauller, vol. II. ; and, lastly, as shown by the writings of *Cochlæus* quoted by *Malvenda,* that damnable Heresiarch yclept Martin Luther.

31. However, with due deference to so many and such erudite Doctors, who are assuredly well agreed upon this circumstance, I can hardly see how their opinion will bear examination. For, as Benedict Pereira, the learned Jesuit, truly observes in his *Commentary on Genesis*, ch. 6, the whole strength and efficiency of the human sperm are contained in the spirits which evaporate and evanish as soon as it issues from the genital vessels wherein it is warmly stored ; all medical men are unanimous as to this. It is consequently not possible that the Demon should preserve in the state essential for generation the sperm he has received ; for it were necessary that whatever vessel he endeavoured to keep it in should be equally warm as the human genital organs, the warmth of which is nowhere to be met with but in those organs themselves. Now, in a vessel where that warmth is not intrinsical but extraneous, the spirits are necessarily altered, and no generation can take place. There is too this other objection, that generation is a vital act by which man, begetting from his own substance, carries the sperm through natural organs to the spot which is appropriate to generation. On the contrary, in this particular case, the introduction of sperm cannot be a vital act of the man who begets, since it is not carried into the womb by his agency ; and, for the same cause, it cannot be said that the man, whose sperm it once was, has begotten the foetus which proceeds from it. Nor can the Incubus be deemed its father, since the sperm does not issue from his

own substance. Consequentially, a child would be born without a father, which is absurd. Third objection : when the father begets in the course of nature, there is a concurrence of two casualties : the one, material, for he provides the sperm which is the matter of generation ; the other, efficient, for he is the principal agent of generation, as all Philosophers maintain. But, in this case, the man who only provided the sperm would contribute but a mere material, without any action tending to generation ; he could not therefore be regarded as the father of the child begotten under such conditions ; and this is clean opposed to the notion that the child begotten by an Incubus is not his son, but the son of the man whose sperm the Incubus has taken.

32. Besides, there is not a shadow of probability in what was written by Valesius and quoted from him by us (*uide supra No.* 30) ; and I am indeed surprised that any thing so extravagantly absurd should have fallen from the pen of such a learned man. Medical men are well aware that the size of the fœtus depends, not indeed on the quantity of matter, but on the quantity of virtue, that is to say of spirits held by the sperm ; therein lies the whole secret of generation, as is well observed by Michael Ettmüller, *Institutiones Medicæ Physiologæ :* " Generation," says he, " entirely depends upon the genital spirit contained within an envelope of thicker matter ; that spermatic matter does not remain in the uterus, and has no share in the formation of the fœtus ; it is but the genital spirit of the male, combined with the

genital spirit of the female, that permeates the pores, or, less frequently, the tubes of the uterus, which it fecundates by that means." What bearing therefore can the quantity of sperm have on the size of the fœtus ? Besides, it is not always a fact that men thus begotten by Incubi are remarkable for the huge proportions of their body : Alexander the Great, for instance, who is said to have been thus born, as we have mentioned, was very short ; and the poet said of him :

Magnus Alexander corpore paruus erat.

Besides, although it is generally a fact that those who are thus begotten excel other men, yet such superiority is not always shown by their vices, but sometimes by their bravery and even their virtues ; Scipio Africanus, for instance, Cæsar Augustus, and Plato the Philosopher, as is recorded of each of them respectively by Livy, Suetonius, and Diogenes Laertius, were men of the highest morality. Whence it may be inferred that, if other individuals begotten in the same way have been wholly evil, it was not owing to the fact that they were born of an Incubus, but rather that they, of their own free will, chose to be bad.

We also read in the Bible, *Genesis*, ch. vi., v. 4, that giants were born when the sons of God went in to the daughters of men : this is the actual text. Now, those giants were men *of great stature*, says *Baruch*, ch. iii., v. 26, and far superior to other men. Not only were they distinguished by their huge size, but also by their physical powers, their rapine and their tyranny. Through their misdeeds the Giants, according to Cornelius à Lapide, in his *Commentary on Genesis*, were the primary and principal cause of the Flood. Some contend that by Sons of God are meant the sons of Seth, and by daughters of men the daughters of Cain, because the former practised piety, religion and every other virtue, whilst the descendants of Cain were quite the reverse; but, with all due deference to S. John Chrysostom, S. Cyril, S. Theodore of Studium, Abbot Rupert of Deutz, S. Hilary and others who are of that opinion, it must be conceded that it hardly agrees with the obvious meaning of the text. Scripture says, in fact, that of the conjunction of the Sons of God and the daughters of men were born men of huge bodily size : consequently, those giants were not previously in existence, and if their birth was the result of that conjunction, it cannot be ascribed to the intercourse of the sons of Seth with the daughters of Cain, who being themselves of ordinary stature, could but procreate children of ordinary stature. Therefore, if the intercourse in question gave birth to beings of huge stature, the reason is that it was not the common connexion between man and woman, but the operation of Incubi who, from their nature, may very well be styled Sons of God. Such is the opinion of the Platonist Philosophers and of Francesco Giorgio the Venetian ; nor is it discrepant from that of Josephus the Historian, Philo Judæus, S. Justin Martyr, Clement of Alexandria, Tertullian, and Hugh of S. Victor, who look upon Incubi as corporeal Angels who have fallen into the sin of lewdness with women. Indeed, as shall be shown hereafter, though seemingly distinct, those two opinions are but one and the same.

33. If therefore these Incubi, as is so commonly held, have begotten Giants by means of sperm taken from man, it is impossible, as aforesaid, that of that sperm should have been born any but men of approximately the same size as he from whom it came; for it would be in vain for the Demon, when acting the part of a Succubus, to draw from man an unwonted quantity of prolific liquor in order to procreate therefrom children of higher stature; quantity is irrelevant, since all depends, as we have said, upon the vitality of that liquor, not upon its quantity. We are bound therefore to infer that Giants are born of another sperm than man's, and that, consequently, the Incubus, for the purpose of generation, uses a semen which is not man's. But what, then, are we to say with regard to this?

34. Subject to correction by our Holy Mother Church, and as a mere expression of private opinion, I say that the Incubus, when having intercourse with women, begets the human fœtus from his own seed.

35. To many that proposition will seem almost heterodox and hardly rational; but I beg of my readers not to condemn it precipitately; for if, as Celsus says, it is improper to deliver judgement without having thoroughly inquired into the law, no less unfair is the rejection of an opinion, before

the arguments upon which it rests have been weighed and confuted. I have therefore to prove the above conclusion, and must necessarily lay down certain premises.

36. Firstly, I premise, as an article of belief, that there are purely spiritual creatures, not in any way partaking of corporeal matter, as was ruled by the Lateran Council, during the pontificate of Innocent III. (S. Firmilian of Cæsarea, S. Cyril, and other authorities confirm this.) Such are the blessed Angels, and the Demons condemned to everlasting fire. Some Doctors, as, for example, Domingo Bañez, Sisto of Siena, Giovanni Pico della Mirandola, Luis de Molina, Bartolomé Carranza, have, it is true, professed, subsequently even to this Council, that the spirituality of Angels and Demons is not an article of belief. Other Doctors, as S. Bonaventura, the Venerable Duns Scotus, Cajetan, Francesco Giorgio, have maintained that they are corporeal, whence Bonaventura Baron (*Scotus Defensus et amplificatus*) has drawn the conclusion that it is neither heretical nor erroneous to ascribe to Angels and Demons a twofold substance, corporeal and spiritual. Yet, the Council having formally declared it to be an article of belief that God *is the maker of all things visible and invisible, spiritual and corporeal, Who has raised from nothing every creature spiritual or corporeal, Angelic or terrestrial,* I contend it is an article of belief that there are certain merely spiritual creatures, and that such are Angels ; not all of them, truly, but a certain number.

37. Perhaps this may seem strange, yet it must be admitted not to be unlikely. If, in fact, Theologians concur in establishing amongst Angels a specific, and therefore essential, diversity, so considerable that, according to S. Thomas, there are not two Angels of the same species, but that each of them is a species by himself, why should not certain Angels be most pure spirits, and consequently of a very superior nature, and others corporeal, and therefore of a less perfect nature, differing thus from each other in their corporeal or incorporeal substance? This doctrine has the advantage of solving the otherwise insoluble contradiction between two Œcumenical Councils, namely the Seventh General Synod and the above-mentioned Council of Lateran. For, during the fifth sitting of that Synod, the Second of Nicea, a book was introduced written by John of Thessalonica against a pagan Philosopher, wherein occur the following propositions: "*Respecting Angels, Archangels and their powers, to which I also adjoin our own Souls, the Catholic Church is indeed of opinion that they are intelligences, but not entirely bodiless and senseless, as you Gentles aver; she on the contrary ascribes to them a subtile body, aerial or igneous, according to what is written: He makes His Angels spirits, and His Ministers a burning fire.*" And later: "*Although not corporeal in the same way as ourselves, made of the four elements, yet it is impossible to say that Angels, Demons, and Souls are incorporeal; for they have been seen many a time, wearing their own body, by those whose eyes the Lord had opened.*" And after that book had been read

through before all the Fathers in Council assembled, Tharasius, the Patriarch of Constantinople, submitted it to the approval of the Council, with these words : " *The Father showeth that Angels should be pictured, since their form can be defined, and they have been seen in the shape of men.*" Without a dissentient, the Synod answered : " *Yea, my Lord.*"

38. That this approbation by a Council of the doctrine set forth at length in the book of John establishes an article of belief with regard to the corporeity of Angels, there is not a shadow of doubt : so Theologians toil and moil in order to remove the contradiction apparent between that decision and the definition, above quoted, by the Council of Lateran. One of them, Suarez, says that if the Fathers did not disprove such an assertion of the corporeity of Angels, it is because that was not the question. Another, Bañez, contends that the Synod certainly approves the conclusion, namely, that Angels might be pictured, but not necessarily the motive given, *their corporeity.* A third, Molina, observes that the definitions issued in Council by the Synod were thus issued only at the *seventh sitting,* whence he argues that those of the previous sittings are not definitions of belief. Others, again, such as Cardinal Cienfuegos and Mirandola, write that neither the Council of Nicea nor that of Lateran intended defining a question of belief, the Council of Nicea having spoken according to the opinion of the Platonists, which describes Angels as corporeal beings, and which was then prevailing, whilst that

of Lateran followed Aristotle, who, in his xiith book of *Metaphysics*, lays down the existence of incorporeal intelligences, a doctrine which has since been adopted by most Doctors in preference to that of the Platonists.

39. But any one can discern the invalidity of such answers, and Bonaventura Baron (*Scot. Defens.*, vol. 9) has no difficulty in showing clearly how unsatisfactory they are. In consequence, that we may make the two Councils agree, we must say that the Council of Nicea meant one species of Angels, and that of Lateran another : the former, corporeal, the latter on the contrary absolutely incorporeal ; and thus are reconciled two otherwise seemingly irreconcilable Councils.

40. Secondly, I premise that the word Angel applies, not indeed to the kind, but to the office : the Holy Fathers are agreed thereupon (S. Ambrose, *On the Epistle to the Hebrews ;* S. Hilary, *On the Trinity*, Book V. ; S. Austin, *City of God ;* St. Gregory, *Homily* 34 *on Scripture ;* S. Isidore, *Supreme Goodness*). An Angel, says S. Ambrose most admirably, is thus styled, not because he is a spirit, but on account of his office: Ἄγγελος in Greek, *Nuntius* in Latin, that is to say *Messenger ;* it follows that whoever is entrusted by God with a mission, be he spirit or man, may be called an Angel, and is indeed thus called in the Holy Scriptures, where the following words are applied to Priests, Preachers, and Doctors, who, as Messengers of God, explain to men the divine will (Malachias, ch. ii., v. 7). "*The*

lips of the priest shall keep knowledge, and they shall seek the law at his mouth, because he is the Angel of the Lord of Hosts." The same prophet, ch. iii., v. 1, bestows the name of Angel on S. John the Baptist, when saying : "*Behold, I send my Angel and he shall prepare the way before my face.*" That this prophecy literally applies to S. John the Baptist is testified by our Lord Jesus Christ, in the Gospel according to S. Matthew, ch. x., v. 10. Yea, more : God himself is called an Angel, because he has been sent by His Father to herald the law of grace. In proof of this we have the prophecy of Isaias, ch. ix., v. 6, according to the Septuagint : "*He shall be called an Angel of Wonderful Counsel.*" And more plainly still in Malachias, ch. iii., v. 1 : "*The Lord whom you seek and the Angel of the testament, whom you desire, shall come to his temple,*" a prophecy which literally applies to our Lord Jesus Christ. There is consequently nothing absurd in the contention that some Angels are corporeal, since men, who assuredly have a body, are called Angels.

41. Thirdly, I premise that neither the existence nor the nature of the natural things in this world have been sufficiently investigated to permit a fact to be denied, merely because it has never been previously spoken of or written about. In the course of time have not new lands been discovered which the Ancients knew not of ? New animals, herbs, plants, fruits and seeds, never seen elsewhere. And if that mysterious Austral land came at last to be explored, as has to this very day been vainly

attempted by so many travellers, what unsuspected discoveries would be the result! Through the invention of the microscope and other instruments used by modern experimental Philosophy, combined with the more exact methods of investigation of Anatomists, have there not been, and are there not, every day, brought to light the existence, qualities and characteristics of a number of natural things unknown to ancient Philosophers, such as fulminating gold, phosphorus, and a hundred other chemical compounds, the circulation of the blood, the lacteal vessels, the lymph-ducts and other recent anatomical discoveries? To deride a doctrine because it does not happen to be mentioned in any ancient author would therefore be absurd, especially bearing in mind this axiom of Logic : *locus ab auctoritate negatiua non tenet.*

42. Fourthly, I premise that Holy Scripture and ecclesiastical tradition do not teach us any thing beyond what is requisite for the salvation of the soul, namely Faith, Hope, and Charity. Consequently, although a thing is not explicitly stated either by Scripture or tradition it must not be inferred that that thing has no existence. For instance, Faith teaches us that God, by His Word, made things visible, and invisible, and also that, through the merits of our Lord Jesus Christ, grace and glory are conferred on every rational creature. Now, that there be another World than the one we live in and that it be peopled by men not born of Adam but made by God, in some other way, as is implied by

those who believe the moon to be inhabited; or further, that in the very World where we dwell, there be other rational creatures besides man and the Angelic Spirits, creatures generally invisible to us and whose being is disclosed but accidentally, through the instrumentality of their own power; all that has nothing to do with Faith, and the knowledge or ignorance thereof is no more necessary to the salvation of man than knowing the number or nature of all physical things.

43. Fifthly, I premise that neither Philosophy nor Theology is repugnant to the possible existence of rational creatures having spirit and body, and distinct from man. Such repugnance could be attributed only to God, and that is inadmissible, since He is almighty, or to the thing to be made, and that likewise cannot be justly attributed; for, as there are purely spiritual creatures, such as Angels; or merely material, such as the World; or lastly semi-spiritual and semi-corporeal, of an earthly and gross corporeity, such as man; so there may well be in existence a creature endowed with a rational spirit and a corporeity less gross, more subtile than man's. There is no doubt, moreover, but that after the Resurrection, the souls of the blessed will be united with a glorified and subtile body; from which it can be inferred that God may well have made a rational and corporeal creature whose body naturally enjoys the subtilty which will be conferred by grace on the glorified body.

44. But, the possible existence of such creatures

will be still better set forth by answering the arguments which can be adduced against our conclusion, and replying to the questions it may raise.

45. First question : Should such creatures be styled rational animals ? And if so, in what do they differ from man, with whom they would have that definition in common ?

46. I reply : Yes, they would be rational animals, provided with senses and organs even as man ; they would, however, differ from man not only in their more subtle nature, but also in the matter of their body. In fact, as is shown by Scripture (*Genesis*, II. 7), man has been made from the grossest of all elements, namely, slime, a gross mixture of water and earth : but those creatures would be made from the most subtle part of all elements, or of one or other of them ; thus, some would proceed from earth, others from water, or air, or fire ; and, in order that they should not be defined in the same terms as man, to the definition of the latter should be added the mention of the gross materiality of his body, wherein he would differ from the said animals.

47. Second question : At what period would those animals have been originated, and whence? From earth, like the beasts, or from water, like quadrupeds, and birds ? Or, on the contrary, would they have been made, like man, by our Lord God ?

48. I reply : It is an article of belief, expressly laid down by the Council of Lateran, that whatever is, in fact and at present, was made at the creation of

the world. By His almighty power, God, at the beginning of time, raised together out of nothing both orders of creatures, spiritual and corporeal. Now, those animals also would be included in the totality of creatures. As to their formation, it might be said that God Himself, through the medium of Angels, made their body as He did man's body, to which an immortal spirit was to be united. That body being of a nobler nature than that of other animals, it was very meet it should be united to an incorporeal and most noble spirit.

49. Third question: Would those animals descend from one individual, as all men descend from Adam, or, on the contrary, would many have been made at the same time, as was the case with the other living things created from earth and water, wherein were males and females for the preservation of the kind by generation? Would there be amongst them a distinction between the sexes? Would they be subject to birth and death, to sense, passions, want of food, power of growth? If so, what are their provisions? Would they lead a social life, as men do? By what laws would they be ruled? Would they build up cities for their dwellings, cultivate the arts and sciences, possess property, and wage war between themselves, as men are wont to do?

50. I reply: It may be that all descend from one individual, as men descend from Adam; it may also be that a number of males and females were made in the beginning, who preserved their kind by generation. We will further admit that they are

born and die; that they are divided into males
and females, and are moved by the senses and passions, as men are; that they feed and grow according to the size of their body; their food, however,
instead of being gross like that required by the
human body, must be delicate and ætherial, emanat-
ing through spiritual essences from whatever in the
physical world abounds with highly volatile cor-
puscles, such as the flavour of meats, especially of
roast, the bouquet of wine, the fragrancy of fruit,
flowers, scents, which emit an abundance of those
effluvia until all their subtile and volatile parts have
completely evaporated. To their being able to lead
a social life, with distinctions of rank and prece-
dence; to their cultivating the arts and sciences,
exercising functions, maintaining armies, building
up cities, as it were; doing in short whatever is
requisite for their preservation, I have in the main
no objections to urge.

51. Fourth question: What would their figure
be, human or otherwise? Would the ordering of
the divers parts of their body be essential, as with
other animals, or merely accidental, as with fluid
substances, such as oil, water, clouds, smoke, etc.?
Would those organic parts consist of various substances, as is the case with the organs of the human
body, wherein are to be found very gross parts, such
as the bones, others less gross, such as the cartilage,
and others slender, such as the membranes?

52. I reply: As regards their figure, we neither
can nor should make over definite assertions, since it

escapes our senses, being too delicate for our sight or our touch. That we must leave to themselves, and to such as have the privilege of intuitive acquaintance with immaterial substances. But, so far as probability goes, I say that their figure tallies with the human body, save there be some distinctive peculiarity, should the very tenuity of their body not be deemed sufficient. I am led to that by this consideration, namely; Of all the works of God the human frame is the most perfect, and that whilst all other animals stoop to the ground, because their soul is mortal, God, as Ovid the poet, says, in his *Metamorphoses* (I. 85–6):

> Os homini sublime dedit, cœlumque tueri
> Iussit, et erectos ad sidera tollere uultus;
> *Gave man an erect figure, bidding him behold the heavens*
> *And raise his face on high towards the stars,*

man's soul having been made immortal for his heavenly home. Considering that the animals we are speaking of would be gifted with a spirit immaterial, rational, and immortal, capable therefore of salvation and damnation, it is proper to admit that the body to which that spirit is united may be like unto the most noble animal frame, that is to say, to the human frame. Whence it follows that in the divers parts of that body there must be an essential order; that the foot, for instance, cannot be an appendage to the head, nor the hand to the belly, but that each organ is in its right place, according to the functions it has to perform. As to the constituent parts of those organs, it is, in my opinion, obvious that there must be some more or less strong, others more or less slender, in order to meet the requirements of the working of the organism. Nor can this be fairly objected to on the ground of the slenderness of the bodies themselves ; · for the strength or thickness of the organic parts alluded to would not be absolute, but merely in comparison with the more slender ones. That, moreover, may be observed in all natural fluids, such as wine, oil, milk, etc. ; however homogeneous and similar to each other their component parts may look, yet they are not so : for some are clayey, others aqueous ; there are fixed salts, volatile salts, brimstone, all of which are demonstrated by a chemical analysis. So it would be in our case : for, supposing the bodies of those animals to be as subtile and slender as the natural fluids, air, water, etc., there would nevertheless be discrepancies in the quality of their constituent parts, some of which would be strong when compared with others more slender, although the whole body which they compose might be called slender.

53. It may be objected that this is repugnant to what was said above concerning the essential ordering of the parts among themselves ; that it is seen that, in fluid and subtile bodies, one part is not essentially but only accidentally connected with another ; that a part of wine, for instance, just now contiguous with some other, soon comes in contact with a third, if the vessel be turned upside down or the wine shaken, and that all the parts together

exchange positions at the same time, though it be still the same wine. Whence it should be inferred that the bodies of those animals would have no permanent figure, and would consequently not be purely organic.

54. I answer that I deny the assumption. In fact, if in fluid bodies the essential ordering of the parts is not apparent, it subsists none the less and causes a compound to preserve its own state. Wine, for instance, when pressed from the grape, seems a thoroughly homogeneous liquor, and yet is not so; for there are gross parts which, by the passage of time, subside in the casks; there are also slender parts which evaporate; fixed parts, such as tartar; volatile parts, such as brimstone and alcohol; others again, half volatile and half fixed, such as phlegm. Those several parts do not respectively maintain an essential order; for no sooner has the must been pressed from the grape, and been styled brimstone or volatile spirits, than it continues so closely involved with the particles of tartar, which is fixed, as not to be in any way able to escape.

55. That is the reason why must recently pressed from the grape is of no use for the distillation of the sulphurous spirits, commonly called *Brandy;* but, after forty days' fermentation, the particles of the wine change places: the spirits, no longer bound up with the tartaric particles which they kept in suspension through their own volatility, whilst they were, in return, kept down by them and prevented from escaping, sever from those particles,

and continue confused with the phlegmatic parts from which they become easily released by the operation of fire, and evaporate : thus, by means of distillation, Brandy is made, which is nothing but the brimstone of wine volatilized by heat with the most slender part of phlegm. At the end of forty days another fermentation begins, which extends more or less, according as the maturity of the wine is more or less perfect, and the termination of which is dependent on the greater or lesser abundance of sulphurous spirits. If abounding with brimstone, the wine sours and turns to vinegar ; if, on the contrary, it holds but little brimstone, it ropes, and becomes what the Italians call *vino molle* or *vino guasto*. If the wine is at once ripe, as happens in other cases, it turns acid or ropes in less time, as is shown by every-day experience. Now, in this said fermentation the essential order of the parts of wine is altered, but not so its quantity nor its matter, which neither changes nor decreases : a bottle that had been filled with wine is, after a certain time, found to be filled with vinegar, without any alteration in its quantity of matter ; the essential order of its parts has alone been modified : the brimstone, which, as we have said, was united to the phlegm and separated from the tartar, becomes again involved and fixed with the tartar ; so that, on distilling the vinegar, there issues from it first an insipid phlegm, and then those spirits of vinegar, which are the brimstone of wine intermixed with particles of tartar that is less fixed. Now, the essential shifting of the aforesaid parts alters the substance of the juice of the grapes, as is clearly shown by the varied and contrary effects of must, wine, vinegar, and ropy or stummed wine ; for which cause the two first are fit, but the two last unfit materials for consecration. We have borrowed the above exposition of the economy of wine from the able work of Nicolas Lémery, chemist to the King of France, *Cours de Chimie*, p. 2, c. 9.

56. If now we apply that natural doctrine to our subject, I say that, being given the corporeity of the animals in question, subtile and slender like the substance of liquids ; being given also their organization and figure, which demand an essential order of the various parts, an adverse hypothesis could raise no argument contrary to their existence ; for, just as the jumbling together of the parts of wine and the diversity of their accidental dispositions do not alter their essential order, even so it would be with the slender frame of our animals.

57. Fifth question : Would those animals be subject to disease and other infirmities which afflict mankind, such as ignorance, fear, idleness, paralysis, etc. ? Would they be wearied through labour, and require, for recruiting their strength, sleep, food, drink ? And what food, what drink ? Would they be fated to die, and might they be killed casually, or by the instrumentality of other animals ?

58. I reply : Their bodies, though subtile, being material, they would of course be liable to decay : they might therefore suffer from adverse agencies,

and consequently be diseased ; that is, their organs might not perform, or painfully and imperfectly perform the office assigned to them, for therein consist all diseases of whatsoever kind with certain animals, as has been distinctly explained by the famous Michael Ettmüller, *Physiology*, ch. v. thesis 1. In sooth, their body being less gross than the human frame, comprising fewer elements mixed together, and being therefore less composite, they would not so easily suffer from adverse influences, and would therefore be less liable to disease than man ; their life would also exceed his ; for, the more perfect an animal, as a species, the longer its days; thus it is with mankind, whose existence extends beyond that of other animals. For I do not believe in the hundred years of crows, stags, ravens and the like, of which Pliny tells his customary stories ; and although his legends have been re-echoed by others without previous inquiry, it is no less clear that before writing thus, not one has faithfully noted either the birth or the death of those animals : they have been content to repeat these idle fables, as has been the case with the Phœnix, whose longevity is rejected as a myth by Tacitus, *Annals*, Book vi. It were therefore to be inferred that the animals we are speaking of would live longer still than man; for, as shall be explained below they would be more noble than he ; consequently also, they would be subject to the other bodily affections, and require rest and food, as mentioned (No. 50). Now, as rational beings amenable to training, they might also continue ignorant, if their minds did not receive the culture and discipline of study and instruction, and some amongst them would be more or less versed in science, more or less clever, according as their intelligence had been more or less educated. However, generally speaking, and considering the whole of the species, they would be more learned than men, not from the subtilty of their body, but probably because of the greater activity of their minds or the longer space of their life, which would enable them to learn more things than men : such are indeed the reasons assigned by S. Augustine (*De diuinatione dæmonum*, ch. 3, and *De Spiritu et anima*, ch. 37), for the prescience of the future in Demons. They might indeed suffer from natural agencies ; but they could hardly be killed, on account of the speed with which they could escape from danger ; it is therefore most unlikely that they could, without the greatest difficulty, be put to death or mutilated by beast or by man, with natural or artificial weapons, so quick would they be to avoid the impending blow. Yet, they might be killed or mutilated in their sleep, or in a moment of inadvertence, by means of a solid body, such as a sword brandished by a man, or the fall of a heavy stone ; for, although subtile, their body would be divisible, just like air which, though vaporous, is yet divided by a sword, a club, or any other solid body. Their spirit, however, would be indivisible, and like the human soul, entire in the whole and in each and every part of the body. Consequently, the division of their body by another body, as aforesaid, might occasion mutilation and even death, for the spirit, itself indivisible, could not animate both parts of a divided body. True, just as the parts of air, separated by the agency of a body, unite again as soon as that body is withdrawn, and constitute the same air as before, even so the parts of the body divided, as above mentioned, might unite and be revived by the same spirit. But in this case it must follow that those animals could not be slain by natural or artificial agencies : and it were more reasonable to maintain our first position ; for, if they share matter with other creatures, it is natural that they should be liable to suffer through those creatures, according to the common rule, and even unto death.

59. Sixth question : Could their bodies penetrate other bodies, such as walls, wood, metals, glass, etc. ? Could many of them abide together on the same material spot, and to what space would their body extend or be restrained ?

60. I answer : In all bodies, however compact, there are pores, as is apparent in metals where, more than in other bodies, it would seem there should be none ; through a perfect and powerful microscope the pores of metals are discerned, with their different shapes. Now, those animals might, through the pores, creep into, and thus penetrate any other bodies, although such pores were impervious to other liquors or material spirits, wine, for example, salts of ammonia, or the like, because their bodies would be much more subtle than those liquors. How-

ever, notwithstanding many Angels may abide together on the same material spot, and even confine themselves in a lesser and lesser space, though not infinitely, as is shown by *Duns Scotus* (2 dist. quest. 6. Ad proposi. et quæst. 8), yet it were rash to ascribe the same power to those animals ; for, their bodies are determined in substance and impervious to each other ; and if two glorious bodies cannot abide together on the same spot, though a glorious and a non-glorious one may do so, as Godfrey of Fontaines maintains (*Quolibet*, q. 5), and Duns Scotus agrees with him (2 distinct. 2, q. 8), much less would it be possible for the bodies of those animals, which are indeed subtile, yet do not attain to the subtility of the glorious body. As regards their power of extension or compression, we may instance the case of air, which, rarefied and condensed, occupies more or less room, and may even, by artificial means, be compressed into a narrower space than would be naturally due to its volume ; as is seen with those large balls which, for amusement, one inflates by means of a blow-pipe or tube : air, being forced into them and compressed, is held in larger quantity than is warranted by the capacity of the ball. Similarly the bodies of the animals we are speaking of might, by their natural virtue, extend to a larger space, not exceeding however their own substance ; they might also contract, but not beyond the determined space consistent with that same substance. And, considering that of their number, as with men, some would be tall and some short, it were proper that the tall should be able to extend more than the short, and the short to contract more than the tall.

61. Seventh question : Would those animals be born in original sin, and have been redeemed by our Lord Jesus Christ? Would grace have been conferred upon them and through what sacraments? Under what law would they live, and would they be capable of salvation and damnation?

62. I answer : It is an article of the Catholic faith that Christ has merited grace and glory for all rational creatures without exception. It is also an article of faith that glory is not conferred on a rational creature until such creature has been previously endowed with grace, which is the disposition to glory. According to a like article, glory is conferred but by merits. Now, those merits are grounded on the perfect observance of the commands of God, and this is accomplished through grace. The above questions are thus solved. Whether those creatures did or did not sin originally is uncertain. It is clear, however, that if their first Parent had sinned as Adam sinned, his descendants would be born in original sin, as men are born. And, as God never leaves a rational creature without a remedy, so long as it treads the way, if those creatures were infected with original or with actual sin, God would have provided them with a remedy ; but whether such be the case, and of what kind is the remedy, is a secret between God and them. Assuredly, if they had Sacraments either identical with or different from those in use in the Church

militant on earth, for the institution and efficacy of these they would be indebted to the merits of Jesus Christ, the Redeemer, who has made perfect Atonement and fullest satisfaction for all rational creatures. It would likewise be highly proper, nay necessary, that they should live under some law given them by God, through the observance of which they might merit salvation; but what would be that law, whether merely natural or written, Mosaic or of the Gospel, or different from all these and specially instituted by God, that we are ignorant of, and know nothing. Yet, whatever it might be, there would follow no objection exclusive of the possible existence of such creatures.

63. The only argument, and that rather a lame one, which long meditation has suggested to me against the possibility of such creatures, is that, if they really existed in the World, we should find them mentioned somewhere by Philosophers, Holy Scripture, Ecclesiastical Tradition, or the Fathers : and since such is not the case, their utter impossibility should be inferred.

64. But that argument which, in fact, calls in question their existence rather than their possibility, is easily disposed of by our premises, Numbers 41 and 42 ; for no argument can stand by force of a negative authority. Besides, it is incorrect to assert that neither the Philosophers, nor the Scriptures, nor the Fathers have handed down any notion of them. Plato, as is reported by Apuleius (*The God of Socrates*) and Plutarch (*Isis and Osiris*), to whom

Bonaventura Baron refers, declared that Demons were beings of the animal kind, passive souls, rational intelligences, aerial bodies, immortal; and he gave them the name of *Demons,* which of itself is nowise offensive, since it means *replete with wisdom ;* so that, when authors allude to the Devil (or Evil Angel), they do not merely call him Demon, but *Cacodemon,* and say likewise *Eudemon,* when speaking of a good Angel. Those creatures are also mentioned in Scripture and by the Fathers, as we will show later.

65. Now that we have proved that those creatures are possible, let us go a step further, and show that they exist. Taking for granted the truth of the recitals concerning the intercourse of Incubi and Succubi with men and beasts, recitals so numerous that it would be sheer impudence to deny the fact, as is said by S. Augustine, whose testimony is given above (No. 10) (*City of God,* xv. 23), I argue: Where the peculiar passion of the sense is found, there also, of necessity, is the sense itself; for, according to the principles of philosophy, the peculiar passion flows from nature, that is to say that, where the acts and operations of the sense are found, there also is the sense, the operations and acts being but its external form. Now, those Incubi and Succubi present acts, operations, peculiar passions, which spring from the senses ; they are therefore endowed with senses. But senses cannot exist without concomitant component organs, without a combination of soul and body. Incubi and Succubi

have therefore body and soul, and, consequentially, are animals ; but their acts and operations are also those of a rational soul; their soul is therefore rational; and thus, from first to last, they are rational animals.

66. Our minor is easy of demonstration in each of its parts. And indeed, the appetitive desire of coition is a sensual desire ; the grief, sadness, wrath, rage, occasioned by the denial of coition, are sensual passions, as is seen with all animals ; generation through coition is evidently a sensual operation. Now, all that happens with Incubi, as has been shown above : they incite women, sometimes even men ; if denied, they sadden and storm, like lovers : *amantes, amentes ;* they practise perfect coition, and sometimes beget. It must therefore be inferred that they have senses, and consequently a body ; consequently also, that they are perfect animals. More than that: in spite of closed doors and windows they enter wherever they please ; their body is therefore slender : they foreknow and foretell the future, compose and divide, all which operations are proper to a rational soul ; they therefore possess a rational soul and are, in fine, rational animals.

Doctors generally reply that it is the Evil Spirit that perpetrates those impure acts, simulates passions, love, grief at the denial of coition, in order to entice souls to sin and to undo them ; and that, if he copulates and begets, it is with assumed sperm and a body not truly his own, as aforesaid (No. 24).

67. But then, there are Incubi that have connexion

with horses, mares and other beasts, and, as shown by everyday experience, ill-treat them if they are averse to coition; yet, in those cases, it can no longer be adduced that the Demon simulates the appetite for coition in order to bring about the ruin of souls, since beasts are not capable of everlasting damnation. Besides, love and wrath with them are productive of quite opposite effects. For, if the loved woman or beast humours them, those Incubi behave very well; on the contrary, they use them most savagely when irritated and enraged by a denial of coition: this is amply proved by daily experience: those Incubi therefore have truly sexual passions and desires. Besides, the Evil Spirits, the incorporeal Demons who copulate with Sorceresses and Witches, constrain them to Demon worship, to the abjuration of the Catholic Faith, to the commission of enchantments, magic, and foul crimes, as preliminary conditions to the infamous intercourse, as has been above stated (No. 11); now, Incubi endeavour nothing of the kind: they are therefore not Evil spirits. Lastly, as Guazzo, who quotes from Peltanus and Thyræus, tells us, at the mere utterance of the Holy Names of Jesus or Mary, at the sign of the Cross, the approach of Holy Relics or consecrated objects, at exorcisms, adjurations or priestly injunctions, the Evil Demon either shudders and takes to flight, or is agitated and howls, as is daily seen with energumens and is shown by numerous narratives of Guazzo concerning the midnight sabbats of Witches, where, at a sign of the Cross or the name of Jesus said by one of the assistants, Devils and Witches all vanish together. Incubi, on the contrary, stand all those ordeals without taking to flight or showing the least fear ; sometimes even they laugh at exorcisms, assault the Exorcists themselves, and rend the sacred vestments. Now, if the evil Demons, subdued by our Lord Jesus Christ, are stricken with fear by His Name, the Cross and the holy things ; if, on the other hand, the good Angels rejoice at those same things, without however inciting men to sin or offend God, whilst the Incubi, without having any dread of the holy things, provoke to sin, it is clear that they are neither evil Demons nor good Angels ; but it is clear also that they are not men, though endowed with reason. What then should they be ? Supposing them to have reached the goal, and to be pure spirits, they would be damned or blessed, for orthodox Theology does not admit of pure spirits on the way to salvation. If damned, they would revere the Name and the Cross of Christ ; if blessed, they would not incite men to sin ; they would therefore be different from pure spirits, and thus, have a body and be on the way to salvation.

68. Besides, a material agent cannot act but on an equally passive material. It is indeed a trite philosophical axiom, that agent and patient must have a common subject : pure matter cannot act on any purely spiritual thing. Now, there are natural agents which act on those Incubi: they are therefore material or corporeal. Our minor is

proved by the testimony of Dioscorides, Book II. ch. 168, and I. ch. 100; Pliny, xv. 4; Aristotle, Problems, XXXIV.; and Apuleius, *De Uirtute Herbarum*, quoted by Guazzo, *Compendium Maleficarum*, Book III., ch. 13, fol. 316; it is confirmed by our knowledge of numerous herbs, stones and animal substances which have the virtue of driving away Demons, such as rue, St. John's wort, verbena, germander, Palma Christi, centaury, diamonds, coral, jet, jasper, the skin of the head of a wolf or an ass, women's menstrue, and a hundred other things : wherefore Guazzo tells us : *For such as are assaulted by the Demon it is lawful to employ stones or herbs, but without recourse to incantations.* It follows that, by their own native virtue, stones or herbs can bridle the Demon : else the above-mentioned Canon would not permit their use, but would on the contrary forbid it as superstitious. We have a striking instance thereof in Holy Scripture, where the Angel Raphael says to Tobias (vi. 8), speaking of the fish which he had drawn from the Tigris : " *If thou put a little piece of its heart upon coals, the smoke thereof driveth away all kinds of devils.*" Experience demonstrated the truth of those words ; for, no sooner was the liver of the fish set on the fire, than the Incubus who was in love with Sara was put to flight.

69. To this Theologians usually retort that such natural agents merely initiate the ejection of the Demon, and that the completive effect is due to the supernatural force of God or of the Angel ; so that the supernatural force is the primary, direct, and

principal cause, the natural force being but secondary, indirect, and subordinate. Thus, in order to explain how the liver of the fish burnt by Tobias drove away the Demon, Valesius asserts that the smoke thereof had been endowed by God with the supernatural power of expelling the Incubus, in the same manner as the material fire of Hell has the virtue of tormenting Demons and the souls of the damned. Others, such as Nicolas of Lyra, Cornelius à Lapide, and Benedict Pereira, believe that the smoke of the heart of the fish initiated the ejection of the Demon by its own native virtue, but completed it by angelical and heavenly virtue : by native virtue, insomuch that it opposed a contrary action to that of the Demon ; for the Evil Spirit applies native causes and humours, the native qualities of which are combated by the contrary qualities of natural things known to be capable of driving away Demons. This opinion is held by all those who treat of the art of exorcism.

70. But that explanation, however plausible the facts upon which it rests, can at most be received as regards the Evil Spirits which possess bodies or, through sheer malice, infect them with diseases and other infirmities ; it does not at all meet the case of Incubi. For these neither possess bodies nor infect them with diseases ; they, at most, annoy them by blows and ill-treatment. If they cause the mares to grow lean because of their not yielding to coition, it is merely by taking away their provender, in consequence of which they fall off and finally die. To

that purpose the Incubus need not use a natural agent, as the Evil Spirit does when imparting a disease : it is enough that he should exert his own native organic force. Likewise, when the Evil Spirit possesses bodies and infects them with diseases, it is most frequently through signs agreed upon with himself, and arranged by a witch or a wizard, which signs are usually natural objects, indued with their own noxious virtue, and, of course, opposed by other equally natural objects endowed with a contrary virtue. But not so the Incubus : it is of his own accord, and without the co-operation of either witch or wizard, that he pursues his molestation. Besides, the natural things which put the Incubi to flight exert their virtue and bring about a result without the intervention of any exorcism or blessing ; it cannot therefore be said that the ejection of the Incubus is initiated by natural, and completed by divine virtue, since there is in this case no particular invocation of the divine Name, but the mere effect of a natural object, in which God co-operates only as the universal agent, the author of nature, the first of efficient causes.

71. To illustrate this important point, I will here relate two stories, the first of which I have from a good confessor of Nuns, a man of integrity and fair repute, and most worthy of credit ; the second I was eye-witness to myself.

In a certain convent of holy Nuns there resided, as a boarder, a young maiden of noble family, who was tempted by an Incubus that appeared to her both

by day and by night, and with the most earnest entreaties, the prayers of a passionate lover crazed for
love, incessantly besought her to lie with him ; but
she, supported by the grace of God and the frequent use of the sacraments, stoutly resisted the
temptation. Yet, notwithstanding all her devo-
tions, fasts and vows, maugre the exorcisms, the
blessings, the injunctions showered by exorcists on
the Incubus that he should desist from molesting
her ; in spite of the vast number of Relics and other
holy objects collected in the maiden's room, of the
lighted candles kept burning there all night, the
Incubus none the less persisted in appearing to her
constantly, in the shape of an exceptionally handsome young man. At last, among other learned
men, whose advice had been taken on the subject,
was a very profound Theologian who, observing
that the maiden was of a thoroughly phlegmatic
temperament, surmised that that Incubus was an
aqueous Demon (there are in fact, as is testified by
Guazzo (*Compendium Maleficarum*, I. 19), igneous,
aerial, phlegmatic, earthly, and subterranean demons
who avoid the light of day), and so he prescribed a
continual suffumigation in the room. A new vessel,
made of earthenware and glass, was accordingly
introduced, and filled with sweet calamus, cubeb
seed, roots of both aristolochies, great and small
cardamom, ginger, long-pepper, caryophylleæ, cin-
namon, cloves, mace, nutmegs, calamite storax,
benzoin, aloes-wood and roots, one ounce of fragrant sandal, and three quarts of half brandy and

water; the vessel was then set on hot ashes in order to force forth and upwards the fumigating vapour, and the cell was kept closed. As soon as the suffumigation was done, the Incubus came, but never dared enter the cell; only, if the maiden left it for a walk in the garden or the cloister, he appeared to her, though invisible to others, and throwing his arms round her neck, stole or rather snatched kisses from her, to her intense disgust. At last, after a new consultation, the Theologian prescribed that she should carry about her person pills and pomanders made of the most exquisite perfumes, such as musk, amber, civet, Peruvian balsam, and other essences. Thus furnished, she went for a walk in the garden, where the Incubus suddenly appeared to her with a threatening face, and in a black rage. He did not approach her, however, but, after biting his finger as if meditating revenge, suddenly disappeared and was never more seen by her.

72. Here is the other story. In the great Carthusian monastery of Pavia there lived a Deacon, Augustine by name, who was subjected by a certain Demon to excessive, unheard-of, and scarcely credible vexations. Many exorcists made repeated endeavours to secure his riddance, yet all spiritual remedies had proved unavailing. I was consulted by the Vicar of the convent, who had the care of the unfortunate cleric. Seeing the inefficacy of all customary exorcisms, and remembering the above-related instance, I advised a suffumigation similar to the one that has been detailed, and prescribed that the young Deacon

should carry about his person fragrant pills and comfits of the same kind; moreover, as he was in the habit of using snuff, and was very fond of brandy, I advised snuff and brandy perfumed with musk. The Demon appeared to him by day and by night, under various shapes, as a skeleton, a pig, an ass, an Angel, a bird; with the figure of one or other of the monks, once even with that of his own Superior the Prior, exhorting him to keep his conscience clean, to trust in God, to confess frequently; he persuaded him to let him hear his sacramental confession, recited with him the psalms *Exsurgat Deus* and *Qui habitat*, and the Gospel according to S. John: and when they came to the words *Uerbum caro factum est*, he genuflected devoutly, then donning a stole which was in the cell, and taking the aspergillum, he blessed with holy water the cell and the bed, and, as if he had really been the Prior, enjoined on the Demon not to venture in future to molest his subordinate; he next incontinently disappeared, thus betraying what he was, for otherwise the young Deacon would have taken him for his Prior. Now, notwithstanding the suffumigations and perfumes I had prescribed, the Demon did not desist from his wonted apparitions; more than that, assuming the features of his victim, he went to the Vicar's room, and asked for some snuff and brandy perfumed with musk, of which, he said, he was extremely fond. Having received both, he vanished in the twinkling of an eye, thus showing the Vicar that he had been mocked by the Demon;

and this was amply confirmed by the Deacon, who affirmed upon his oath that he had not gone that day to the Vicar's cell. When these circumstances were told to me, I inferred that, far from being aqueous like the Incubus who was in love with the maiden above spoken of, this Demon was igneous, or, at the very least, aerial, since he delighted in hot substances such as warm vapours, perfumes, snuff and brandy. My surmises were greatly confirmed by the temperament of the young Deacon, which was choleric and sanguine, choler, however, somewhat predominating; for these Demons never approach any save those whose temperament tallies with their own. And this is another confirmation of my views regarding their corporeity. I therefore advised the Vicar to let the junior monk take herbs that are cold by nature, such as water-lily, agrimony, spurge, mandrake, house-leek, plantain, henbane, and others of a similar family, knit two little bundles of them and hang them up, one at his window, the other at the door of his cell, taking care to strow some also on the floor and on the bed. Marvellous to say! the Demon appeared again, but remained outside the room, which he would not enter; and, on the Deacon inquiring of him his motives for such unwonted reserve, he burst out into invectives against me for giving such advice, disappeared, and never returned thither again.

73. The two stories I have related make it clear that, by their native virtue alone, perfumes and herbs drove away Demons without the intervention

of any supernatural force ; Incubi are therefore subject to material conditions, and it must be inferred that they participate of the matter of the natural objects which have the power of putting them to flight, and consequently they have a body ; which is what was required to be demonstrated.

74. But, the better to establish our conclusion, it behoves us to correct the mistake into which have fallen the Doctors quoted above, such as Valesius and Cornelius à Lapide, when they say that Sara was freed from the Incubus by the power of the Angel Raphael, and not by that of the fish callionymus caught by Tobias on the banks of the Tigris. Indeed, saving the respect due to such great doctors, their construction manifestly clashes with the clear meaning of the Text, from which it is never justifiable to deviate, so long as it does not lead to absurd consequences. Here are the words spoken by the Angel to Tobias : " *If thou put a little piece of its heart on coals, the smoke thereof driveth away all kinds of devils, either from man or from woman, so that they come no more to them, and the gall is good for anointing the eyes in which there is a white speck, and they shall be cured* " (*Tobias*, ch. vi. vv. 8 and 9). We must notice that the Angel's assertion respecting the virtue of the heart, or liver, and gall of that fish is absolute, universal ; for, he does not say : " *If thou puttest on coals little pieces of its heart, thou wilt put to flight all kinds of devils, and if thou anointest with its gall eyes in which there is a white speck, they shall be cured.*" If he had thus spoken, I could agree with the con-

struction that S. Raphael had brought about, by his own supernatural power, the effects which the mere application of the smoke and the gall might not have been enough to produce: but he does not speak thus, nay, on the contrary, he says absolutely, that such is the virtue of the smoke and the gall.

75. It may be asked whether the Angel spoke the precise truth regarding the virtue of those things, or whether he might have lied; and likewise, whether the white speck was withdrawn from the eyes of the elder Tobias by the native force of the gall of the fish, or by the supernatural virtue of the Angel S. Raphael? To say that the Angel could have lied would be an heretical blasphemy; he therefore spoke the precise truth; but it would no longer be so if all kinds of Demons were not expelled by the smoke of the liver of the fish, unless aided by the supernatural force of the Angel, and especially, if such aid was the principal cause of the effect produced, as the Doctors assert in the present case. It would doubtless be a lie if a physician should say: such an herb radically cures pleurisy or epilepsy, and if it should only begin the cure, the completion of which required the addition of another herb to the one first used; in the same manner, S. Raphael would have lied when averring that the smoke of the liver expelled all kinds of devils, so that they should not return, if that result had been only begun by the smoke, and its completion had been principally due to the power of the Angel. Besides, that flight of the devil was either

to take place universally, and by the act of any one whosoever might put the liver of the fish on the coals, or else it was only to occur in that particular case, when the younger Tobias put the liver on the coals. In the first hypothesis, any person making that smoke by burning the liver should be assisted by an Angel, who, through his supernatural virtue would expel the Devils miraculously and regularly at the same time; which is absurd; for, either words have no meaning, or a natural fact cannot be regularly followed by a miracle; and, if the Devil was not put to flight without the assistance of the Angel, S. Raphael would have lied when ascribing that virtue to the liver. If, on the contrary, that effect was only to be brought about in that particular case, S. Raphael would again have lied when assigning to that fish, universally and absolutely, the virtue of expelling the Demon : now, to say that the Angel lied is not possible.

76. The white speck was withdrawn from the eyes of the elder Tobias, and his blindness healed, through the native virtue of the gall of that same fish, as many Doctors aver (Nicolas of Lyra, Dionysius, and the authorities quoted by Cornelius à Lapide in his glosses on *Tobias*, vi. 9). In fact, that the gall of the fish callionymous, which the Italians call *bocca in capo*, and of which Tobias made use, is a highly renowned remedy for removing whiteness from the eyes, all are agreed; Dioscorides, Galen, Pliny, and Valesius. The Greek Text of *Tobias*, ch. xi, v. 13, says: " *He poured the gall on his father's eyes,*

saying : Have confidence, father ; but there being erosion the old man rubbed his eyes, and the scales of the whiteness came out at the corners." Now, since, according to the same text, the Angel had disclosed to Tobias the virtue of the liver and gall of the fish, and since, through its native virtue, the gall cured the elder Tobias's blindness, it must be inferred that it was likewise through its native force that the smoke of the liver put the Incubus to flight ; which inference is conclusively confirmed by the Greek text, which, *Tobias*, ch. viii, v. 2, instead of the reading in the Vulgate : " *He laid a part of the liver on burning coals,*" (*Protulit de cassidili suo partem iecoris, posuitque eam super carbones uiuos*), says explicitly : " *He took the ashes of the perfumes, and put the heart and the liver of the fish thereupon, and made a smoke therewith ; the which smell when the evil spirit had smelled, he fled.*" The Hebrew text says : " *Asmodeus smelled the smell, and fled.*" From all those texts it appears that the Devil took to flight on smelling a smoke which was prejudicial and hurtful to himself, and nowise did he flee from the supernatural power of the Angel. If, in ridding Sara from the assaults of the Incubus Asmodeus, the operation of the smoke of the liver was followed by the intervention of S. Raphael, it was in order to bind the Demon in the desert of Upper Egypt, as related, *Tobias*, ch. viii, v. 3 ; for, at such a distance, the smoke of the liver could neither operate on the Devil, nor bind him. And here we have the means of reconciling our opinion with that of the above-mentioned Doctors, who

ascribe to S. Raphael's power Sara's complete riddance from the Devil: for, I say with them, that
the cure of Sara was completed by the binding of
the Devil in the wilderness, the deed of the Angel;
which I concede; but I maintain that the deliver-
ance properly called, that is to say, the ejection from
Sara's bed-chamber, was the direct effect of the
virtue of the liver of the fish.

77. A third principal proof of our conclusion
regarding the existence of those animals, in other
words, respecting the corporeity of Incubi, is adduced by the testimony of S. Jerome, in his *Life of
S. Paul, the first Hermit.*   S. Antony, says he, set on
a journey to visit S. Paul.   After travelling several
days, he met a Centaur, of whom he inquired the
hermit's abode; whereupon the Centaur, growling
some uncouth and scarcely intelligible answer,
pointed the direction with his out-stretched hand,
and then fled with the utmost speed into a wood.
The Holy Abbot kept on his way, and, in a dene,
met a little man, almost a dwarf, with taloned hands,
horned brow, and his lower extremities ending in
the feet of a goat.   At such a sight S. Antony stood
still, and fearing the arts of the Devil, comforted
himself with a great sign of the Cross. But, far from
running away, or even seeming frightened at it, the
little fellow respectfully approached the old man,
and tendered him, as it were a peace offering, dates
as refreshment for his journey.   The blessed S.
Antony having then inquired who he was: "*I am
a mortal,*" replied he, "*and one of the inhabitants of*

the Wilderness, whom the Pagans, in their many blind errors, worship under the names of Fauns, or Satyrs, or Incubi. I am on a mission from my people : we beg thee to pray for us unto the common God, whom we know to have come for the Salvation of the world, and whose Praises are sounded all over the earth." Rejoicing exceedingly at the glory of Christ, S. Antony, turning his face towards Alexandria, and striking the ground with his staff, cried out : *" Woe be unto thee, thou harlot City, who worshipest animals as Gods ! "* Such is the narrative of S. Jerome, who dwells at length on the fact, explaining its import in an ample discourse.

78. It were indeed rash to doubt the truth of the above recital, constantly referred to by the greatest of the Doctors of the Holy Church, S. Jerome, whose authority no Catholic will ever deny. Let us therefore investigate these circumstances which most clearly must confirm our opinion.

79. Firstly, we observe that if ever a Saint was assailed by the arts of the Demon, saw through his infernal devices, and carried off victories and trophies from the contest, that Saint was S. Antony, as is shown by his life written by S. Athanasius. Now, since in that little man S. Antony did not recognize a devil, but an animal, saying : *" Woe be unto thee, thou harlot City, who worshipest animals as Gods ! "*, it is clear that it was no devil or pure spirit ejected from heaven and damned, but some kind of animal. Still more : S. Antony, when instructing his friars and cautioning them against the assaults of

the Demon, said to them, as related in the Roman Breviary, 17 January (*Feast of S. Antony, Abbot, II Nocturn, lection vi.*) : " *Believe me, my brethren, Satan dreads the vigils of pious men, their prayers, fasts, voluntary poverty, compassion and humility ; but, above all, he dreads their burning love of our Lord Jesus Christ, at the mere sign of whose most Holy Cross he flies away disabled.*" As the little man, against whom S. Antony guarded himself with a sign of the Cross, neither took fright nor fled, but approached the Saint confidently and humbly, offering him some dates, it is a sure sign that he was no Devil.

80. Secondly, we must observe that the little man said : " *I also am a mortal,*" whence it follows that he was an animal subject to death, and consequently called into being through generation ; for, an immaterial spirit is immortal, because simple, and consequently is not called into being through generation from pre-existent matter, but through creation, and, consequently also, cannot lose it through the corruption called death ; its existence can only come to an end through annihilation. Therefore, when he said he was mortal, he professed himself an animal.

81. Thirdly, we must observe that he acknowledged he knew that the God of all had suffered in human flesh. Those words show him to have been a rational animal, for brutes know nothing but what is sensible and present, and can therefore have no knowledge of God. If that little man said that he and his fellows were aware that God had suffered in

human flesh, it shows that, by means of some revelation, he must have acquired the knowledge of
God, as we have ourselves the revealed Faith. That
God assumed human flesh and suffered in it, is the
essence of the two principal articles of our Faith :
the existence of God one and threefold, His Incarnation, Passion and Resurrection. All that shows,
as I said, that it was a rational animal, capable of the
knowledge of God through revelation, like ourselves, and endowed with a rational, and consequently, immortal soul.

82. Fourthly, we must observe that, in the name
of his whole race whose delegate he professed to
be, he besought S. Antony to pray for them to
the common God of all. Whence I infer that that
little man was capable of salvation and damnation,
and that he was not *in termino* but *in uia ;* for, from
his being, as has been shown above, rational and
consequently endowed with an immortal soul, it
follows that he was capable of salvation and damnation, the proper lot of every rational Creature,
Angel or man. I likewise infer that he was on the
way, *in uia,* that is, capable of merit and demerit ;
for, if he had been at the goal, *in termino,* he would
have been either blessed or damned. Now, he
could be neither the one nor the other ; for, S.
Antony's prayers, to which he commended himself, could have been of no assistance to him, if
finally damned, and, if actually saved, he stood in
no need of them. Since he commended himself to
the Saint's prayers, it shows they could be of avail

to him, and, consequently, that he was on the way to salvation, *in statu uiæ et meriti.*

83. Fifthly, we must observe that the little man professed to be delegated by others of his kind, when saying : " *I am on a mission from my race,*" words from which many inferences may be deduced. One is, that the little man was not alone of his kind, an exceptional and solitary monster, but that there were many of the same species, since congregating they made up a race, and that he came in the name of all ; which could not have been, had not the will of many been represented by, and centred in him. Another is, that those animals lead a social life, since one of them was sent in the name of many. Another again is, that, although living in the Wilderness, it is not assigned to them as a permanent abode ; for S. Antony having never previously been in that desert, which was far distant from his hermitage, they could not have known who he was nor how great his degree of sanctity ; it was therefore necessary that they should have become acquainted with him elsewhere, and, consequently, that they should have travelled beyond that wilderness.

84. Lastly, we must observe that the little man said he was one of those whom *the Pagans, blinded by error, call Fauns, or Satyrs, or Incubi :* and by these words is shown the truth of our principal proposition : that Incubi are rational animals, capable of salvation and damnation.

85. The apparition of such little men is of fre-

quent occurrence in metallic mines, as is noted by
George Agricola in his book *De Animantibus subterraneis.* They suddenly appear to the miners,
clothed like miners themselves, play and jump out
together, laugh and titter, and flip little stones at
them in joke : a sign, says the above-named Author,
of excellent success, and of the finding of some
branch or body of a mineral tree.

86. Peter Thyræus, of Neuss, in his book *De
Terrificationibus nocturnis,* denies the existence of such
little men, and supports his denial upon the following truly puerile arguments : given such little men,
says he, how do they live, and where do they dwell ?
How do they propagate their kind, through generation or otherwise ? Are they born, do they die,
upon what meat do they feed ? Are they capable of
salvation and damnation, and by what means do
they procure their salvation ? Such are the arguments upon which Thyræus relies to support his
denial of their existence.

87. But it really shows little judgement in a man
to deny that which has been written by grave and
credible Authors, and is confirmed by everyday
experience. Thyræus's arguments are worthless and
have been already refuted, Nos. 45 and following. The only question which remains to be
answered is this : Where do those little men, or
Incubi, dwell ? To that I reply : As has been shown
above (No. 71), according to Guazzo, some are
earthly, some aqueous, some aerial, some igneous,
that is to say, their bodies are made of the most

subtle part of one of the elements, or, if of the combination of many elements, that yet there is one which predominates, either water or air, according to their nature. Their dwellings will consequently be found in that element which is preponderant in their bodies : igneous Incubi, for instance, will only stay when compelled, may be will not stay at all, in water or marshes, which are adverse to them ; and aqueous Incubi will not be able to rise into the upper part of ether, the subtlety of which region is repugnant to them. We see the like happen to men who, accustomed to thicker air, cannot endure certain lofty ridges of the Alps where the air is too subtle for their lungs.

88. Many testimonies of Holy Fathers, gathered by Molina, in his *Commentary on St. Thomas*, would go to prove the corporeity of Demons ; but, taking into account the above-quoted decision of the Council of Lateran (No. 36), concerning the incorporeity of Angels, we must understand that the Holy Fathers had in view those Incubi which are still on the way to salvation, and not those demons that are damned. However, to cut matters short, we merely give the authority of S. Augustine, that eminent Doctor of the Church, and it will be clearly seen how thoroughly his doctrine harmonizes with ours.

89. S. Augustine, then, in his *Commentary on Genesis*, Book II., ch. 17, writes as follows concerning Demons : " *They have the knowledge of some truths, partly through the more subtle acumen of their senses,*

partly through the greater subtilty of their bodies," and, Book III., ch. 1 : *" Demons are aerial animals, because they partake of the nature of aerial bodies."* In his Epistle 115, to Hebridius, he affirms that they are *" aerial or ethereal animals, endowed with very acute intelligence."* In the *City of God*, Book XI., ch. 13, he says that *" even the worst Demon has an ethereal body."* Book XXI., ch. 10, he writes : *" The bodies of certain Demons, as has been believed by some learned men, are even made of the thick and damp air which we breathe."* Book XV., ch. 23 : *" I dare not explicitly decide whether Angels, with an ethereal body, can feel the lust which would incite them to copulate with women."* In his Commentary on Psalm lxxxv., he says that *" the bodies of the blessed will, after resurrection, be like unto the bodies of Angels "* ; on Psalm xiv., he observes that *" the body of Angels is inferior to the soul."* And, in his book *De Diuinatione Dæmonum*, he everywhere, and especially in ch. XXIII., teaches that *" Demons have very subtle bodies."*

90. Our view can also be confirmed by the testimony of the Holy Scriptures, which, however diversely construed by commentators, yet patently affirm our proposition. First, Psalm lxxvii., vv. 24 and 25, it is said : *" The Lord had given them the bread of heaven ; Man ate the bread of angels."* David here alludes to manna, which fed the children of Israel during the whole time that they wandered in the wilderness. It will be asked in what sense it can be said of manna that it is the *Bread of Angels*. I am aware that most Doctors construe this passage

in a mystical sense, saying that manna figures the
Holy Eucharist, which is styled the *Bread of Angels*,
because Angels enjoy the sight of God who, by con-
comitance, is found in the Eucharist.

91. A most proper construction assuredly, and
it is adopted by the Church in the office of Corpus
Christi ; but it is in a spiritual sense. Now what I
seek is the literal sense ; for in that Psalm David
does not speak, as a prophet, of things to be, as he
does in other places where a literal sense is not easily
to be gathered ; he speaks here as a historian, of
things gone by. That Psalm, as is evident to any
reader, is a plain epitome, or summing up of all the
benefits conferred by God on the Hebrew People
from the exodus out of Egypt to the days of David,
and the manna of the Wilderness is spoken of in it ;
how, and in what sense is manna then styled the
Bread of Angels ? that is the question.

92. I am aware that many writers, for example,
Nicolas of Lyra, the Blessed Robert Bellarmine,
Francis Titelmann, Gilbert Genébrand, and others,
look upon the Bread of Angels as bread prepared by
Angels, or sent down from Heaven by the ministry
of Angels. But Cardinal Hugh of St.-Cher explains
that qualification by saying that this food partly
produced the same effect upon the Jews, which the
food of Angels produces upon the latter. Angels,
in fact, are not liable to any infirmity ; on the other
hand Hebrew commentators, and Josephus himself,
assert that whilst in the Wilderness, living upon
manna, the Jews neither grew old, nor sickened,

nor tired ; so that manna was actually in its effects like unto the bread that Angels feed upon, for they know neither old age, nor disease, nor any weariness.

93. These interpretations should indeed be received with the respect due to the authority of such eminent Doctors. There is, however, one difficulty in this : namely that, by the ministry of Angels, the pillars of the cloud and fire, the quails, and the water from the rock were provided for the Hebrews, no less than the manna ; and yet they were not styled the pillar, the water or the beverage of Angels. Why therefore should manna be called *Bread of Angels*, because provided by their ministry, when the qualification *Drink of Angels* is not given to the water drawn from the rock likewise by their ministry ? Besides, in Holy Scripture, when it is said of bread that it is the *bread of somebody*, it is always the *bread of him* who feeds on it, not of him who provides or makes it. Of this there are numberless instances : thus, *Exodus*, xxiii. 25 : "*That I may bless your bread and your waters*" ; *Kings*, book II., xii. 3 : "*Eating of his bread*" ; *Tobias*, iv. 17 : "*Eat thy bread with the hungry*," and v. 18 : "*Lay out thy bread on the burial of a Just Man*" ; *Ecclesiastes*, xi. 1 : "*Cast thy bread upon the running waters*" ; *Isaias*, lviii. 7 : "*Deal thy bread to the hungry*" ; *Jeremias*, xi. 19 : "*Let us put wood on his bread*" ; *S. Matthew*, xv. 26 : "*It is not good to take the bread of the children*"; *S. Luke*, xi. 3 : "*Our daily bread.*" All those passages clearly show that, in Scripture, the bread of somebody is

the bread of him who feeds upon it, not of him who makes, brings, or provides it. In the passage of the Psalm we have quoted, *Bread of Angels* may therefore easily be taken to mean the food of Angels, not incorporeal indeed, since these require no material food, but corporeal, that is to say of those rational animals we have described of, who live in the air, and, from the subtlety of their bodies and their rationality, approximate so closely to immaterial Angels as actually to fall under the same denomination.

94. I conclude then that, being animals, consequently reproducible through generation and liable to corruption, they require food for the restoration of their corporeal substance wasted by effluvia : for the life of every sensible being consists in nothing else but the motion of the corporeal elements which flow and ebb, are acquired, lost, and recruited by means of substances spirituous, yet material, assimilated by the living thing, either through the inhalation of air, or by the fermentation of food which spiritualizes its substance, as is shown by that great scholar Ettmüller (*Instit. Medic. Physiolog.*, ch. 2).

95. But, their body being subtile, equally subtile and delicate must be its food. And, just as perfumes and other vaporous and volatile substances, when adverse to their nature, offend and put them to flight, as testified by what we related above (Nos. 71 and 72), in the like manner, when agreeable, they delight in and feed upon them. Now, as is written by Cornelius à Lapide, " *Manna is nothing but an*

emanation of water and earth, refined and baked by the heat of the sun, and then coagulated and condensed by the cold of the following night " ; of course, I am speaking of the manna sent down from Heaven for the nourishment of the Israelites, and which wholly differs from our modern medicinal manna in use to-day ; for this, in fact, according to Ettmüller (*Dilucid. Physiol.*, ch. 1), *" is merely the juice or transudation of certain trees which, during the night, gets mixed up with dew, and, the next morning, coagulates and thickens in the heat of the sun."* The manna of the Israelites, on the contrary, derived from other principles, far from coagulating, liquefied in the heat of the sun, as is shown by Scripture, *Exodus*, xvi., 21 : *" After the sun grew hot, it melted."* The manna of the Israelites was therefore undoubtedly of a most subtile substance, consisting as it did of emanations of earth and water, and being dissolved by the sun it disappeared : consequently, it may very well have been the food of the animals we are speaking of, and thus have been truly called by David *Bread of Angels*.

96. We have another authority in the Gospel according to S. John, x. 16, where it is said : *" And other sheep I have, that are not of this fold : them also I must bring, and they shall hear my voice, and there shall be one fold and one shepherd."* If we inquire what are those sheep that are not of this fold, and what is the fold of which Our Lord Jesus Christ speaketh, we are answered by all Commentators that the only fold of Christ is the Church to which the preaching of the Gospel was to bring the Gentiles, sheep of

another fold than that of the Jews. They are, in fact, of opinion that the fold of Christ was the Synagogue, because David had said, Psalm xciv. 7 : *"We are the people of his pasture, and the sheep of his hand,"* and also because Abraham and David had been promised that the Messiah should be born of their race, because He was expected by the Jews, foretold by the Prophets who were Jews, and that His Advent, His acts, His Passion, Death and Resurrection were prefigured in the sacrifices, worship, and ceremonials of the Jewish law.

97. But, saving always the reverence due to the Holy Fathers and other Doctors, that explanation does not seem quite exhaustive. For it is an article of belief that the Church of the Faithful has been the only one in existence from the beginning of the world, and will thus endure to the end of time. The Head of that Church is Jesus Christ, the Mediator between God and men, by Whom all things were created and made. Indeed, faith in the Holy Trinity, though less explicitly, and the Incarnation of the Word were revealed to the first man, and by him taught his children, who, in their turn, taught them to their descendants. And thus, although most men had strayed into idolatry and deserted the true faith, many kept the faith they had received from their fathers, and observing the laws of nature, stayed in the true Church of the Faithful, as is noticed by Cardinal Francisco Toledo, S.J., in reference to Job, who was a saint among idolatrous Gentiles. And, although God had conferred

especial favours upon the Jews, prescribed for them peculiar laws and ceremonials, and separated them from the Gentiles, yet those laws were not obligatory on the Gentiles, and the faithful Jews did not constitute a Church different from that of the Gentiles who professed their faith in one God, and looked for the coming of the Messiah.

98. And thus it came to pass that even among the Gentiles there were some who prophesied the advent of Christ and the other dogmas of the Christian faith, to wit *Balaam*, *Mercurius Trismegistus*, *Hydaspes*, and the *Sibyls* mentioned by Lactantius, Book I., ch. 6, as is remarked by the Venerable Cesare Baronius, in his *Annals*, 18. That the Messiah was expected by the Gentiles is shown by many passages of Isaias, and plainly testified by the prophecy of Jacob, the Patriarch, thus worded, Genesis, xlix. 10 : " *The sceptre shall not be taken away from Juda, nor a ruler from his thigh, till he come that is to be sent, and he shall be the expectation of nations.*" Likewise in the prophecy of Aggeus ii. 8 : " *I will move all Nations, and the Desired of all Nations shall come* " ; which passage is thus commented upon by Cornelius à Lapide : " *The Gentiles before the advent of Christ, who believed in God and observed the natural law, expected and desired Christ equally with the Jews.*" Christ Himself disclosed and manifested Himself to the Gentiles as well as to the Jews ; for, at the same time as the Angel announced His Nativity to the shepherds, by means of the miraculous star He called the Magi to worship Him, and they, being Gentiles,

were the first among the Nations, as the shepherds among the Jews, to acknowledge and worship Christ (*Uide* S. Fulgentius, *Sermon* vi., *upon the Epiphany*). In like manner, the advent of Christ was made known by preaching (I am not speaking of the Apostles) to the Gentiles before it was to the Jews. As is written by the Venerable Mother, Sister Maria d'Agreda, in her *Life of Jesus Christ and the Blessed Virgin Mary :* " *When the Blessed Virgin Mary, fleeing with S. Joseph, from the persecution of Herod, carried the Infant Jesus into Egypt, she tarried there seven years ; and, during that time the Blessed Virgin herself preached to the Egyptians the faith of the true God and the advent of the Son of God in human flesh.*" Besides, the Nativity of Christ was attended by numerous prodigies, not only in Judæa, but also in Egypt, where the idols tumbled down and the oracles were hushed; in Rome, where a spring of oil gushed forth, a golden globe was seen to descend from the skies on earth, three suns appeared, and an extraordinary aureole, variegated like a rainbow, encircled the disc of the sun ; in Greece, where the oracle of Delphi was struck dumb, and Apollo, asked the reason of his silence by Augustus, who was offering up a sacrifice in his own palace where he had raised an altar to him, answered :

> Me puer Hebræus, Diuos Deus ipse gubernans,
> Cedere sede iubet, tristemque redire sub orcum ;
> Aris ergo dehinc tacitis abscedito nostris.

" *A Hebrew child, who sways the Gods, and himself a God,*
" *Bids me quit my seat and return to the infernal regions ;*
" *Depart therefore from our altars, henceforward mute.*"

So Nicephorus, I. 17 ; Suidas, and Cedrenus in his *Compendium Historiæ* relate.

There were many more prodigies warning the Gentiles of the advent of the Son of God : they have been collected from various Authors, by Baronius, and are to be found in his *Annals*, and by Cornelius à Lapide in his *Commentary upon Aggeus*.

99. From all this it is clear that the Gentiles also belonged, as well as the Jews, to the fold of Christ, that is, to the same Church of the Faithful ; it cannot therefore be correctly said that the words of Christ : " *Other sheep I have, which are not of this fold*," are exclusively applicable to the Gentiles, who had, in common with the Jews, the faith in God, the hope, prophecy, expectation, predictive pro- digies and preaching of the Messiah.

100. I therefore maintain that by the words *other sheep* may very well be understood those rational Creatures or animals of whom we have been treating hitherto. They are, as we have pointed out, capable of salvation and damnation, and Jesus Christ is the Mediator between God and man, wherefore every rational Creature (for rational creatures attain to salvation in consideration of the infinite merits of Christ, through the grace He confers upon them, without which salvation is impossible of attainment), every rational creature, I say, must have cherished, at the same time as the faith in one God, the hope of the advent of Christ, and have had the revelation of His Nativity in the flesh and of the principles of the law of grace. Those were therefore the sheep

which were not *of that human fold*, and which Christ had to bring ; the sheep which were to hear His voice, that is, the announcement of His advent and of the evangelical doctrine, either directly through Himself, or through the Apostles ; the sheep which, partaking with men of heavenly bliss, were to realize *one fold and one shepherd*.

101. To this interpretation, which I hold to be in no way improper, force is added by what we related, according to S. Jerome, of that little man who requested S. Antony to *pray*, for him and his fellows, unto the common God, whom he knew to have suffered in human flesh. For, it implies that they were aware of the advent and of the death of Christ, whom, as God, they were anxious to propitiate, since they sought, to that effect, the intercession of S. Antony.

102. Thereto tends also the fact mentioned by Cardinal Baronius (*Annals*, 129), quoting Eusebius of Cæsarea, *Præparatio Euangelica*, v. 9, and Plutarch *De Defectu Oraculorum*, as being one of the prodigies which took place at the time of the death of Christ. He relates that in the reign of the Emperor Tiberius, when Christ suffered, whilst mariners bound from Greece to Italy, were by night, and during a calm, in the vicinity of the Isles of the Echinades, their ship hulled not far from shore. All the crew then heard a loud voice calling upon Tramnus, the master of the ship. When he had answered to his name, the voice replied : " What time thou art hard by such a marsh, announce that *the great Pan is dead*."

This Tramnus did, and there arose suddenly, as from a numberless multitude, groans and shrieks. Doubtless, they were Demons, or corporeal Angels, or rational animals living near the marsh on account of their aqueous nature, and who, hearing of the death of Christ, described by the name of Great Pan, burst into tears and wailed, like some of the Jews who, after witnessing the death of Christ, went home smiting their breasts (*S. Luke*, xxiii. 48). From all that has been concluded above, it is therefore clear that there are such Demons, Succubi and Incubi, endowed with senses and subject to the passions thereof, as has been shown ; who are born through generation and die through corruption, who are capable of salvation and damnation, more noble than man, by reason of the greater subtilty of their bodies, and who, when having intercourse with humankind, male or female, fall into the same sin as man when copulating with a beast, which is inferior to him. Also, it not unfrequently occurs that those Demons slay the men, women, or mares with whom they have had long protracted intercourse ; and the reason is that, being liable to sin whilst on the way to salvation, *in uia*, they must likewise be open to repentance ; and, in the same manner as a man, who habitually sins with a beast, is enjoined by his confessor to destroy that beast, with a view to suppressing the occasion of relapsing, it may likewise happen that the penitent Demon should slay the animal with which it sinned, whether man or beast ; nor will death thus occasioned to a man be reckoned a sin to the Demon, any more than death inflicted on a beast is imputed as a sin to man ; for, considering the essential difference between a Demon of that kind and man, the man will be the same thing to the Demon as the beast is to man.

103. I am aware that many, perhaps most of my readers, will say of me what the Epicureans and some Stoic Philosophers said of S. Paul (*Acts of the Apostles*, xvii. 18). "*He seemeth to be a setter forth of new gods*," and will deride my doctrine. But they will none the less have to answer the foregoing arguments, to show what are those Incubi Demons, commonly called *Goblins*, who dread neither exorcisms, nor holy objects, nor the Cross of Christ, and they must explain the various effects and phenomena we have related when we were propounding that doctrine.

104. What we have hitherto concluded accordingly solves the question laid down Nos. 30 and 34, to wit : how a woman can be got with child by an Incubus Demon ? In fact, it cannot be brought about by sperm assumed from a man, agreeably to the common opinion, which we confuted, Nos. 31 and 32 ; it follows, therefore, that she is directly impregnated by the sperm of the Incubus, who, being an animal and capable of breeding, has sperm of his own. And thus is fully explained the begetting of Giants from the intercourse of the Sons of God with the Daughters of men : for that intercourse gave birth to Giants who, although like

to men, were of higher stature, and, though begotten by Demons, and consequently of great strength, yet equalled their sires neither in might nor in power. It is the same with mules, which are intermediate, as it were, between the kinds of animals from whose promiscuousness they are sprung, and which excel indeed the most imperfect, but never equal the most perfect: thus, the mule excels the ass, but does not attain the perfection of the mare, which has begotten it.

105. In confirmation of the above conclusion, we observe that animals sprung from the mixing of different kinds do not breed, but are barren, as is seen with mules. Now we do not read of Giants having been begotten by other Giants, but rather of their having been born of the Sons of God, that is Incubi, and the Daughters of men : so being thus begotten of the demoniac sperm mixed with the human sperm, and being, as it were, an intermediate species between the Demon and man, they had no generative power.

106. It may be objected that the sperm of Demons, which must, by nature, be most fluid, could not mix with the human sperm, which is thick, and that, consequently, no generation would ensue.

107. I reply that, as has been said above, No. 32, the generative power lies in the spirit that comes from the generator at the same time as the spumy and viscous matter ; it follows that, although most liquid, the sperm of the Demon, being neverthe-

less material, can very well mix with the material spirit of the human sperm, and bring about generation.

108. It will be alleged in answer that, if the generation of Giants had really come from the combined sperms of Incubi and women, Giants would still be born in our time, since there is no lack of women who have intercourse with Incubi, as is shown by the Acts of S. Bernard and S. Peter of Alcantara, and by other examples related in various authors.

109. I reply that, as has been said above, No. 71, from Guazzo, some of those Demons are earthly, some aqueous, some aerial, some igneous, and they all dwell in their respective element. Now, it is well known that animals are of larger size, according to the element they live in ; and it is the same with fishes, many of which are diminutive, it is true, as happens with animals that live on land ; but, the element water being larger than the element earth, since the container is always larger than the contents, fishes as a species, surpass in size the animals that dwell on land, as shown by whales, tunnies, cachalots, saw-fish, sharks, and other cetaceous and viviparous fish which far surpass in size all animals that live on land. Consequently, these Demons being animals, as has been shown, their size will be proportionate to the extent of the element they dwell in, according to their nature. And, air being more extensive than water, and fire than air, it follows that ethereal and igneous Demons will

far surpass their earthly and aqueous fellows, both in stature and might. It would be to no purpose to instance, as an objection, birds which, although inhabitants of the air, a more extensive element than water, are smaller, as a species, than fishes and quadrupeds; for, if birds do indeed travel through the air by means of their wings, they no less belong to the element earth, where they rest; otherwise, some fishes that fly, such as the sea-swallow, would have to be classed among aerial animals, which is not the case.

110. Now, it must be observed that, after the Flood, the air which surrounds our earthy and aqueous globe, became, from the damp of the waters, thicker than it had been before; and, damp being the principle of corruption, that may be the reason why men do not live as long as they did before the Flood. It is also on account of that thickness of the air that ethereal and igneous Demons, who are more corpulent and gross than the others, can no longer dwell in that thick atmosphere, and if they must descend into it occasionally, do so only when obliged, much as divers descend into the depths of the sea.

111. Before the Flood, when the air was not yet so thick, Demons came upon earth and had intercourse with women, thus procreating Giants whose stature was nearly equal to that of the Demons, their fathers. But now it is not so: the Incubi who approach women are aqueous and of small stature; that is why they appear in the shape of little men,

and, being aqueous, they are most lecherous. Lust
and damp go together : Poets have depicted Venus
as born of the sea, in order to show, as is explained
by Mythologists, that lust takes its source in damp.
When, therefore, Demons of short stature impreg-
nate women nowadays, the children that are born
are not giants, but men of ordinary size. It should,
moreover, be known that when Demons have carnal
intercourse with women in their own natural body,
without having recourse to any disguise or artifice,
the women do not see them, or if they do, see but
an almost doubtful, vague, barely sensible shadow,
as was the case with the female we spoke of, No. 28,
who, when embraced by an Incubus, scarcely
felt his touch. But, when they want to be seen by
their mistresses, and to taste to the full the joys of
human copulation, they assume a visible disguise
and a palpable body. By what means this is effected,
is their secret, which our circumscribed Philosophy
is unable to discover. The only thing we know is
that such disguise or body could not consist merely
in concrete air, since this must take place through
condensation, and therefore by the influence of
cold ; a body thus formed would feel like ice, and
in the venereal act could afford women no pleasure,
but would give them pain ; and it is the reverse that
takes place.

112. The distinction being admitted between
wholly spiritual Demons, who have intercourse
with witches, and Incubi, who have to do with
women that are nowise witches, we must now

inquire into the heinousness of the crime in both cases.

113. The intercourse of witches with Demons, from its accompanying circumstances, apostasy from the Faith, the worship of the Devil, and so many other abominations as related above, Nos. 12 to 24, is the greatest of all sins which can be committed by man; and, considering the hideous enormity against Religion which is presupposed by coition with the Devil, Demoniality is assuredly the most grievous of all carnal offences. But, taking the sins of the flesh as such, exclusive of the sins against Religion, Demoniality should be reduced to simple pollution. The reason, a most convincing one, is that the Devil who swives a witch is a pure spirit, has reached the goal and is damned, as has been said above; if, therefore, he copulates with witches, it is in a body assumed or made by himself, according to the common opinion of Theologians. Though set in motion, that body is not a living one; and it follows that the human being, male or female, who has connexion with such a body, is guilty of the same offence as if he copulated with an inanimate body or a corpse, which would be simple pollution, as we have shown elsewhere. It has, moreover, been truly observed by Cajetan, that such intercourse can very well carry with it the guilt of other crimes, according to the body assumed by the Devil, and the member used : thus, if he should assume the body of a kinswoman, or of a nun, such a crime would be incest or sacrilege ; if coition took

place in the shape of a beast, or *in uase præpostero*, it would be Bestiality or Sodomy.

114. As for intercourse with an Incubus, wherein is to be found no element, no, not even the least, of offence against Religion, it is hard to discover a reason why it should be more grievous than Bestiality and Sodomy. For, as we have said above, if Bestiality is more grievous than Sodomy, it is because man degrades the dignity of his kind by mixing with a beast, of a kind much inferior to his own. But, when copulating with an Incubus, it is quite the reverse : for the Incubus, by reason of his rational and immortal spirit, is equal to man ; and, by reason of his body, more noble because more subtile, so he is more perfect and more dignified than man. Consequently, when having intercourse with an Incubus, man does not degrade, but rather dignifies, his nature ; and, taking that into consideration, Demoniality cannot be more grievous than Bestiality.

115. It is, however, commonly held to be more grievous, and the reason I take to be this : that it is a sin against Religion to hold any communication with the Devil, either with or without a compact, for instance by habitually or familiarly companying with him, by asking his assistance, counsel or favour, or by seeking from him the revelation of things to be, the knowledge of the past, of absent things, or of circumstances otherwise hidden. Thus, men and women, by mixing with Incubi, whom they do not know to be animals but believe to be devils, sin

through intention, *ex conscientia erronea*, and their sin is in intention the same, when having intercourse with Incubi, as if such intercourse took place with devils ; wherefore the guilt of their crime is exactly the same.

FINIS

APPENDIX

THE manuscript of *Demoniality* breaks off with the conclusion just given. In a purely philosophical and theoretical acceptation, the work is complete : for it was enough that the author should define, in general terms, the grievousness of the crime, without concerning himself with the proceedings which were to make out the *proof*, or with the *penalty* to be inflicted. Both those questions, on the contrary, had, as a matter of course, a place assigned to them in the great work *De Delictis et Pœnis*, which is a veritable *Code for the Inquisitor ;* and Father Sinistrari of Ameno could not fail to treat them there with all the care and conscientiousness he has so amply shown in the foregoing pages.

The reader will be happy to find here that practical conclusion to *Demoniality*.

(Note by Isidore Liseux.)

PROOF OF DEMONIALITY

SUMMARY

1. *Distinctions to be made in the proof of the crime of Demoniality.*

2. *Signs proving the intercourse of a Witch with the Devil.*

3. *The frank confession of the Sorcerer himself is requisite for a full conviction.*

4. *Tale of a Nun who copulated with an Incubus.*

5. *If the indictment is supported by the recitals of eye-witnesses, torture may be resorted to and employed.*

1. As regards the proof of that crime, a distinction must be made of the kind of Demoniality, to wit : whether it is that which is practised by Witches or Wizards with the Devil, or that which other persons perform with Incubi.

2. In the first case, the compact entered into with the Devil being proved, the evidence of *Demoniality* follows as a necessary consequence ; for, the purpose, both of Witches and Wizards, in the midnight sabbats that take place, after feasting and dancing, is none other but that infamous intercourse ; moreover there can be no witness of that crime, since the Devil, visible to the Witch, escapes the sight of all beside. Sometimes, it is true, women have been seen in the woods, in the fields, in groves and dingles, lying on their backs, naked to their very

navels, in the posture of venery, all their limbs quivering with the orgastic spasm, as is noted by Guazzo, book I., chap. 12, v. *Sciendum est sæpius*, fol. 65. In such a case there would be a very strong suspicion of this crime, particularly if supported by other signs ; and I am inclined to believe that such a circumstance, sufficiently proved by good witnesses, would justify the Judge in resorting to torture in order to ascertain the truth ; especially if, shortly after that action, a sort of black smoke had been seen to issue from the woman, and she had been noticed to rise, as is also noted by Guazzo ; for it might be inferred that that smoke or shadow had been the Devil himself, fornicating with the woman. Likewise if, as has more than once happened, according to the same author, a woman had been seen to fornicate with a mysterious stranger, who, when the action was over, suddenly disappeared.

3. Again, in order to prove conclusively that a person is a Wizard or a Witch, the actual confession of such person is requisite : for there can be no witnesses to the fact, unless perhaps other Sorcerers giving evidence at the trial against their accomplices ; and from their being confederates in the crime, their statement is not conclusive and does not justify the recourse to torture, should not other indications be forthcoming, such as the seal of the Devil stamped on their body, as aforesaid, No. 23, or the finding in their dwelling, after a search, of signs and instruments of the diabolic art : for

example, bones and, especially, a skull, hair artfully plaited, intricate knots of feathers, wings, feet or skeletons of bats, toads, or serpents, unfamiliar and, perhaps, noxious seeds, wax figures, vessels filled with unknown powder, oil or viscid ointments, etc., as are usually detected by Judges who, upon a charge being brought against Sorcerers, proceed to their apprehension and the search of their houses.

4. The proof of copulation with an Incubus offers the same difficulty ; for, no less than other Demons, the Incubus is, at will, invisible to all but his mistress. Yet, it has not seldom happened that Incubi have allowed themselves to be surprised in the act of carnal intercourse with women, now in one shape, now in another.

In a certain Convent (I mention neither its name nor that of the town where it is situate, so as not to recall to memory a past scandal), there was a Nun, who, as is usual with women and especially with nuns, had quarrelled about some silly trifles with one of her sister-nuns, the occupant of the cell adjoining hers. Quick at observing all the doings of this religious with whom she was at loggerheads, our neighbour noticed that, several days in succession, instead of walking with her companions in the garden after dinner she retired to her cell, where she locked herself in with unwonted precautions. Curious to know what she could be doing there all that time, the inquisitive Nun betook herself to her own cell. Presently she heard a sound, as of two voices conversing in subdued tones (which she could easily do, since the two cells were divided but by a slight partition), then a certain noise, the creaking of a bed, groans and sighs, as of two lovers in an orgasm of love. Her wonderment was now raised to the highest pitch, and she redoubled her attention in order to ascertain who was in the cell. But when, three times running, she had seen no other nun come out save her rival, she strongly suspected that a man had been secretly introduced and was kept hidden there. She went accordingly and reported the whole thing to the Abbess, who, after taking counsel with the Discreets, resolved that she would herself listen to the sounds and observe the strange happenings which had been thus denounced to her, so as to avoid any hasty or inconsiderate act. In consequence, the Abbess and her confidents repaired to the cell of the informer, and thence heard the voices and other noises that had been described. Inquiry was made to ascertain whether any of the Nuns could be shut in with this other one; and when this was found not to be the case, the Abbess and her attendants went to the door of the closed cell, and knocked repeatedly, but to no purpose: the Nun neither answered, nor opened. The Abbess threatened to have the door broken in, and even ordered a lay-sister to force it with a crow-bar. The Nun then opened her door: a search was made and no one found. Being asked with whom she had been talking, and the why and wherefore of the bed creaking, of the long-drawn sighs, etc., she denied everything.

But, since matters went on just the same as before, the rival Nun, becoming slyer and more inquisitive than ever, contrived to bore a hole through the partition, so as to be able to discover exactly what was happening inside the cell; and what should she espy but a comely youth lying with the Nun, a sight she took good care to let the others enjoy by the same means. An accusation was soon laid before the Bishop : the guilty Nun still endeavoured to deny all ; but at last, threatened with the torture, she confessed to having been long indecently intimate with an Incubus.

5. When, therefore, indications are forthcoming, such as those detailed above, a charge might be brought after a searching inquiry ; yet, without the confession of the accused, the offence should not be regarded as fully proven, even if the intercourse were actually beheld by eye-witnesses ; for it sometimes happens that, in order utterly to undo an innocent female, the Devil feigns such intercourse by means of some glamour or delusion. In those cases, the Ecclesiastical Judge therefore must trust but to his own eyes alone.

PENALTIES

With regard to the penalties applicable to *Demoniality*, there is no law that I know of, either civil or canonical, which inflicts a punishment for a crime of that kind. Since, however, such a crime implies a compact and communion with the Devil, and apostacy from the faith, not to speak of the evil deeds, damage, and other almost numberless outrages perpetrated by Sorcerers, as a rule it is punished, out of Italy, by the gallows and the stake. But, in Italy, it is very seldom that offenders of this kind are delivered up by the Holy Inquisition to the secular power.

NOTES

P. 1. JUAN CARAMUEL.—Juan Caramuel y Lobkowitz, the famous Spanish theologian, was born at Madrid 23 May 1606 ; and died at Vigevano, 8 September, 1682. At an early age he joined the Cistercian Order, and having already been long famous for his learning, in 1638 he was created a Doctor of Theology by the University of Louvain. He filled in turn the dignities of Abbot of Melrose (Scotland), Abbot-Superior to the Benedictines of Vienna, and Grand-vicar to the Archbishop of Prague. He was elected Bishop of Konig-ratz, then Archbishop of Otranto, and at his death was Bishop of Vigevano.

His knowledge was encyclopædic, and, according to Paquot (*Memoires pour servir l'histoire litteraire des dix-sept provinces des pays-Bas*, Louvain, 1765–70, II., 175), he published no less than 262 works which seem to deal with all the arts and sciences. Especially celebrated is his *Theologia moralis ad prima atque clarissima principia reducta*, Louvain, 1643, a work which, although often spoken against and misunderstood, is of lasting value. S. Alphonsus Liguori has called Caramuel " the Prince of the Laxists."

P. 1. CAJETAN.—Tomaso de Vio Gaetani, Dominican Cardinal, philosopher, theologian, and exegete ; was born 20 February, 1469, at Gaeta ; and died 9 August, 1534, at Rome. His career was most notable, and he has been described as small in bodily stature but gigantic in intellect. It is said that he could quote from memory almost the entire Summa, and by Pope Clement VII. he was called " the Lamp of the Church." In Theology Cajetan is regarded as one of the foremost defenders and exponents of the Thomistic school. His commentaries on the *Summa Theologica*, the first in that extensive field, begun in 1507 and finished 1522, are his greatest work, and they were immediately recognised to be a classic in Scholastic literature. There are very many editions of the commentaries, sometimes including the text of the *Summa*, and sometimes without it. It is noteworthy, however, that Leo XIII. ordered these commentaries to be incorporated with the text of the *Summa* in the official Leonine edition of the works of S. Thomas, the first volume of which appeared at Rome in 1882.

P. 1. SILVESTER.—Francesco Silvester, a famous Dominican theologian, was born at Ferrara about 1474, and died at Rennes 19 September, 1526. He filled the highest offices in his order, being appointed Vicar-general by Clement VII., and on 3 June, 1525, in the general chapter held at Rome, he was elected Master-general. He wrote many theological works of great value, and he is especially praised for the clearness and elegance of his style.

BONACINA.—Martino Bonacina, was an Oblate of S. Ambrose and S. Charles. He is regarded as one of the leading moral theologians of his age, and his works have several times been republished. He died suddenly in 1631, whilst on his way to fill the position of Nuncio of Urban VIII. at the court of the Emperor Ferdinand II. In Theology Bonacina is a Probabilist.

P. 2. VINCENZO FILLIUCCI.—Vincenzo Filliucci, S.J., was born at Siena in 1566, and died at Rome 5 April, 1622. He entered the Society of Jesus at the age of eighteen, and after a brilliant career he was summoned to Rome to fill the chair of Moral Theology in the Roman College, where he taught for ten years with great distinction. His writings on moral theology have frequently been reprinted in various countries, and his authority is justly regarded as ranking very high. He was violently attacked by the Jansenists, and Pascal in his *Lettres Provinciales* makes great capital out of garbled quotations from the many works of this eminent author.

P. 2. ALEXANDER VII.—Twenty-eight propositions derived from the works of the most extreme Laxists were condemned by Alexander VII. 24 September, 1665. Of these the twenty-fourth proposition is as follows :—" Mollities, Sodomia, Bestialitas sunt peccata eiusdem speciei infimæ ; ideoque sufficit in confessione dicere se procurasse pollutionem." (" Masturbation, Sodomy, Bestiality, are sins of the same species ; and therefore it is sufficient for a penitent to say in confession that he has committed self-abuse.") For these sins belong to separate species.

P. 4. GABRIEL VASQUEZ.—Gabriel Vasquez, S.J., the famous theologian, was born at Villæscusa de Haro, near Belmonte, Cuenca, in 1549 or 1551 ; and died at Alcala, 23 September, 1604. His career was most distinguished, and for six years he lectured on moral theology at Rome. Benedict XIV. calls him " the Luminary of Theology." His views on Grace and the Sacrifice of the Mass are famous. In particular he maintained very sound opinions on the Sacrament of Matrimony. Several of his discussions, however, have been disputed, and not without reason. Uir fuit acerrimo ingenio.

P. 4. HENRIQUEZ.—Enrique Henriquez, a noted Jesuit Theologian, born 1536; died 1608. His chief work is *Theologiæ Moralis Summa*, published at Salamanca, 1591. S. Alphonsus highly esteems the authority of Henriquez on moral questions. The second work of Henriquez, *De Pontificis Romani Claue*, libri IV., Salamanca, 1593, is excessively rare, as it was severely censured, and nearly all the copies burned.

P. 4. MEDINA.—Bartholomew Medina, a Dominican theologian, was born at Medina 1527, and died at Salamanca 1581. Practically his whole life was devoted to teaching theology at this latter town. He is usually called the " Father of Probabilism." But it seems more likely that he was merely formulating the teaching on this point when he wrote : " It seems to me that if an opinion is probable, it may be followed, even though the opposite opinion be more probable " (I-II., quest. 19, art. 6).

P. 6. EPISCOPAL CAPITULARIES.—The Capitularies or Capitula of Bishops were compilations of Ecclesiastical law, a summary of previous legislation epitomized for the clergy and people. Some capitularies were applicable to many dioceses, others seem to have been intended for one diocese alone. Among the most famous Capitularies are the capitula of S. Martin, Metropolitan of Braga (571-80); the capitula of S. Boniface (died 754); the *Confessionale* and *Pænitentiale* of Ecgberht, Archbishop of York (735-51); for separate dioceses we have a very great number of capitularies, especially those of Hincmar, Archbishop of Reims (845-82). The capitularies enjoyed great authority throughout the earlier Middle Ages.

The Council of Ancyra was held in 314, and its Canons form a very important document in the early history of the Sacrament of Penance. They were adopted by many canonists and are maintained by Regino of Prüm. Pope S. Damasus I. reigned from 366 to 11 December, 384. Under him various Roman synods were held, and the papal decretals greatly increased in prestige.

LORINUS OF AVIGNON, S.J., born 1559, is famous for his vast commentaries upon the Bible.

P. 7. FRANCESCO MARIA GUAZZO.—Francesco Maria Guazzo, a member of the congregation of S. Ambrose ad Nemus, a local Milanese order, and a writer of extraordinary learning, published his encyclopædic *Compendium Maleficarum* at Milan 1608, second edition 1626. The reader may refer to *The History of Witchcraft* (1926) by the present editor for an account of, and quotations from, Guazzo's work. He is certainly one of the most valuable of the earlier writers.

PAUL GRILLAND.—The author of a valuable treatise, *De Sortilegiis*, published at Lyons in 1533.

NICOLAS REMY (Remigius).—Born 1554, died at Nancy 1600. A magistrate of Lorraine, the "Torquemada lorrain," and Procureur-general under Duke Henri II. An all-important figure in the witch trials of that period. He is the author of a well-known work, *Dæmonolatriæ libri tres*, Lyons. 4to, 1595.

S. PETER DAMIAN.—Cardinal-bishop of Ostia, Doctor of the Church, born 1007; died at Fænza 21 February, 1072.

ALFONSO À CASTRO.—A Franciscan theologian, confessor to Charles V. and Phillip II; was born in 1495 at Zamora, Leon, Spain; and died at Brussels 11 February, 1558. Among his chief works are *Aduersus omnes hæreses*, first edition Cologne, 1539; and *De Iusta Hæreticorum punitione*, Salamanca 1547.

P. 7. PIERRE CRESPET.—A monk of the Celestine order, a mystical and ascetic writer, the author of *Deux livres de la haine de Satan et des malins esprits contre l'homme*, Paris, 1590.

BARTOLOMEO SPINA.—A Dominican theologian, Master of the Sacred Palace under Paul III. He was born at Pisa about 1475, and died at Rome in 1546. Probably his most famous work is the *Tractatus de Strigibus et Lamiis*, Venice, 1523, which has been often reprinted.

GIOVANNI LORENZO ANANIA.—The author of *De Natura dæmonum : libri iv.*, Venice, 1581. 8vo.

P. 8. THE CROWN (Coroncina; chaplet).—The rosary was delivered by Our Lady to S. Dominic, and is the great devotion of the Dominican order. See the Bull of S. Pius V., *Consueuerunt*, 17 September, 1569; also the *Vida di Santo Domingo* (Madrid, 1721) by Blessed Francisco de Possadas, O.P.

S. Francis girded himself with a rough rope in memory of the bonds wherewith Christ was bound during His passion, and a white girdle with three knots has since formed part of the Franciscan habit. Sixtus IV., by his Bull, *Exsuperna dispositionis*, erected the archconfraternity of the cord of S. Francis in the basilica of the Sacro Convento at Assisi, enriching it with many indulgences, favours which have been confirmed by pontiff after pontiff. Archconfraternities are erected not only in Franciscan, but in many other churches and aggregated to the centre at Assisi.

The Archconfraternity of Our Lady of Consolation, or of the Black Leathern Belt of S. Monica, S. Augustine and S. Nicolas of Tolentino, took its rise from a vision of S. Monica, who received a black leathern belt from Our Lady. S. Augustine, S. Ambrose, and S. Simplicianus all wore such a girdle, which forms a distinctive feature of the dress of Augustinian Eremites. After the canonization of S. Nicolas of Tolentino it came into general use as an article of devotion, and Eugenius IV., in 1439, erected the above Archconfraternity. A Bull of Gregory XIII., *Ad ea* (15 July, 1575) confirmed this and added various privileges and indulgences. The Archconfraternity is erected in Augustinian sanctuaries, from the General of which Order leave must be obtained for its extension to other churches.

The Scapular of Our Lady of Mount Carmel is the especial devotion of the Carmelite Order. The Blessed Virgin appeared to S. Simon Stock at Cambridge on Sunday, 16 July, 1251, and presenting him with the brown scapular, made him a particular promise, which is wont to be summed up in the words, " Whoever wears the scapular until death will be preserved from hell, and I will deliver him from Purgatory on the Saturday after his death." This promise was confirmed by the Bull *Sacratissimo uti Culmine* of John XXII., 3 March, 1322, which is known as the Sabbatine Privilege. There are many other scapulars, such as the scapular of the Most Blessed Trinity; of Our Lady of Ransom; of the Mother of Good Counsel; of the Immaculate Heart of Mary; the Black Servite scapular; the Black Passionist scapular; the Blue scapular; the Red scapular; the scapular of S. Joseph; the scapular of S. Michael; of S. Benedict, and very many more.

P. 9. BLACK BOOK.—These books or rolls were in charge of the chief officers of a district. They were guarded with the utmost care, since, as they contained the damning evidence of a full list of the witches belonging to any province, county, or district, their security was a matter of life or death. The signing of such a book is continually referred to in the New England Trials at the end of the seventeenth century. There is a somewhat vague story, no dates being given, that a Devil's book (a list of local witches) was carried off by a certain Mr. Williamson, who stole it whilst the witches were dancing on Minchmoore, Peebles. However, they at once gave chase to him and he was glad to abandon it and escape with his life.

This roll of witches must not be confused with books of charms and spells, nor with what we may term the Devil's Missal, which is used by Satanists in their blasphemous rites.

P. 13. CŒLIUS RHODIGINUS.—Lodovico Ricchieri, the famous Italian philologist, surnamed Rhodiginus from Rovigo (*Rhodigium*), where he was born about 1450, and where he died in 1525. His *Antiquarum lectionum, lib. xvi.*, was published at Venice, folio, 1516 ; Paris, folio, 1517. A more complete edition, comprising thirty books, was issued under the care of Camillo Ricchieri and Goretti at Bale, folio, 1550. I have used the folio Geneva edition of 1620, where the story to which Sinistrari refers will be found in column 1614. It arises from the discussion : *Quæ sit adagii ratio, Serpentem foues, & te serpens. Inibi de lamiis mirum.* Menippus Lycius, a youth of twenty-five, dwelt at Corinth, in a suburb of which city the Lamia was supposed to reside.

The story is originally from Philostratus, *Uita Apollonii*, IV. Keats's exquisite poem *Lamia*, written in 1819, and published with *Isabella, The Eve of S. Agnes, and other Poems* in 1820, is founded upon this legend as related by Burton, *The Anatomy of Melancholy*, Part III., Sect. 2, Memb. 1, Sub-s. 1.

" Philostratus in his fourth book, *de vita Apollonii*, hath a memorable instance in this kind, which I may not omit, of one Menippus Lycius, a young man twenty-five years of age, that going between Cenchreas and Corinth, met such a phantasm in the habit of a fair gentelwoman, which taking him by the hand, carried him home to her house in the suburbs of Corinth, and told him she was a Phœnician by birth, and if he would tarry with her, ' he should hear her sing and play, and drink such wine as never any drank, and no man should molest him ; but she being fair and lovely, would live and die with him, that was fair and lovely to behold.' The young man, a philosopher otherwise staid and discreet, able to moderate his passions, though not this of love, tarried with her awhile to his great content, and at last married her, to whose wedding, amongst other guests, came Apollonius, who, by some probable conjectures, found her out to be a serpent, a lamia, and that all her furniture was like Tantalus's gold described by Homer, no substance, but mere illusions. When she saw herself descried, she wept, and desired Apollonius to be silent, but he would not be moved, and thereupon she, plate, house, and all that was in it, vanished in an instant : many thousands took notice of this fact, for it was done in the midst of Greece."

P. 13. HECTOR BOECE.—Chronicler, and one of the founders of Aberdeen University, 1465–1536. The impetus he gave to historical studies at Aberdeen was of lasting effect. His works are highly esteemed.

Scotorum Historiæ, VIII.—I have used the first edition, 1526, where this story and other similar adventures may be read, folios cliv.–v. " In Gareotha regione, uico quatuordeum uix passuū millibus ab Aberdonia, adolescēs multa formositate, coram Aberdoneñ antistite questus est palam, sese a dęmone Succuba (vt dicunt) gratissima omniū quę uidisset forma, multo antea menses infestatum eandē occlusis foribus noctu ad si ingredi blanditiis, in sui amplexus cōpellere. Dubia luce abiri sine strepitu pœne, nullo se posse modo quū plures attentasset a tāta, actā turpi uesania liberari. Iubet cōtinus optimus episcopus adolescētē, alio se cōferre, & vt christiana religiōe magis laudatis, ieiuniis & oronibus plus solito accōmodaret uim : fore vt piis operibus incēto, uictus cacodemon tādē terga esset daturus. Euenit adolescēti salubre cōsiliū religiose_exequuto, paucos post dies vti uenerādus antistes erat pfatus."

P. 13. FOLLETTI.—Cf. Burton, *Anatomy of Melancholy*, Part I., Sec. 2, Memb. 1, Sub-s. 2.—" Terrestrial devils are those Lares, Genii, Fauns, Satyrs, Wood-nymphs, Foliots, Fairies, Robin Goodfellows, Trulli, &c., which as they are most conversant with men, so they do them most harm . . . some put our fairies into this rank, which have been in former times adored with much superstition, with sweeping their houses, and setting of a pail of clean water, good victuals, and the like, and then they should not be pinched, but find money in their shoes, and be fortunate in their enterprises."

P. 14. PAVIA.—The Largo di Santa Croce leads into the Piazza Castello.

San Michele, where the Kings were crowned, is one of the most remarkable churches in North Italy, and it has been described as the most notable monument of Lombard Architecture.

P. 17. PIUS V.—Michele Ghisleri, O.P., 1504-1572; elected Pope 7 January, 1566. He was beatified by Clement X. in 1672, and canonised by Clement XI. in 1712. He is closely connected with Pavia, for he founded there the Collegio Ghisleri, in front of which stands his statue in bronze.

P. 20. BLESSED BERNARDINE.—Blessed Bernardine of Feltre, Friar minor, 1439-1494. He died at Pavia on 28 September. His body, which lies in the church of S. James, is much venerated. His feast (duplex minus) is kept by the Franciscans on 28 September.

P. 21. BELLARMINE.—Blessed Robert Francis Romolo Bellarmine, S.J., the famous theologian, writer and Cardinal, 1542-1621.

FRANCISCO SUAREZ.—Doctor Eximius, 1548-1617. One of the greatest theologians of the Church.

THOMAS MALVENDA.—O.P., 1566-1628. He was distinguished for the profundity of his theological and philosophical learning. One of his most famous works is the *De Antichristo*, libri XI., Rome, 1604. A truly profound and noble volume.

FRANCISCUS VALESIUS.—Franciscus Valesius, a Spanish Doctor of Physic, flourished towards the end of the sixteenth century. He won a great reputation for his translations of, and commentaries upon, the older medical writers.

P. 22. MALVENDA.—I have used the first edition of the *De Antichristo*, folio, Rome, 1604. The passages quoted by Sinistrari are from Book II., c. IX. (pp. 77-9), whose rubric is : *Aliquot clarissimi uiri apud Gentiles, quos proditum est ex diis, hoc est ex incubis dæmoniis genitos.*

Malvenda thus concludes the chapter : " Et ne simus iam Lectori fastidio, eiusmodi aliis ex tam impuro ortu procreatis recensendis, satis sit indicasse Aristomenem Messenium etiam ex incubo natum, ut Strabo de Situ Orbis, lib. 8, & Pausanias lib. 3 affirmant: cui post mortem repertum esse cor pilosum auctor est Plinius lib. 11, c. 37. Item Merlinum seu Melkinum Anglicum uatem, de quo mirandæ fabulæ narrantur, ex dæmonio incubo & filia Caroli magni Sacra uirgine genitū produnt. Deniq. Lutherum ex incubum ortum, ex Coclæo iam superius annotauimus."

P. 22. ROMULUS AND REMUS.—Livy, I., 2, writes : "Ui compressa uestalis cum geminum partum edidisset, seu ita rata, seu quia deus auctor culpæ honestior erat, Martem incertæ stirpis patrem nuncupat." PLUTARCH ROMULUS, 2, is far more detailed : οἶδε μυθώδη παντάπασι περὶ τῆς γενέσεως διεξώσι. Ταρχετίῳ γαρ Ἀλβαῦων βασιλεῖ παρανομωτάτῳ καὶ ὠμοτάτῳ φάσμα δαιμόνιον οἴκοι γενέσθαί φαλλὸν γὰρ ἐκ τῆς ἑστίας ἀνασχεῖν καὶ διαμένειν ἐπὶ πολλὰς ἡμέρας· εἶναι δὲ Τηθύος ἐν Τυρρηνίᾳ χρηστήριον, ἀφ' οἷ κομισθῆναι τῷ Ταρχετίῳ χρησμὸν, ὥστε συμμῖξαι τῷ φάσματι παρθένον· ἔσεσθαι γὰρ ἐξ αὐτῆς παῖδα κλεινότατον, ἀρετῇ καὶ τύχῃ καὶ ῥώμῃ διαφέροντα. Φράσαντος οὖν τὸ μάντευμα του Ταρχετίου μιᾷ τῶν θυγατέρων καὶ συγγενέσθαι τῷ φαλλῷ προστάξαντος, αὐτὴν μὲν ἀπαξιῶσαι, θεράπαιναν δὲ εἰσπέμψαι, τόνδε Ταρχέτιον, ὡς ἔγνω, χαλεπῶς φέροντα συλλαβεῖν μὲν ἀμφοτέρας ἐπὶ θανάτῳ· τὴν δ' Ἑστίαν ἰδόντα κατὰ τοὺς ὕπνους ἀπαγορεύουσαν αὐτῷ τὸν φόνον, ἱστόν τινα παριγγυῆσαι ταῖς κόραις ὑφαίνειν δεδεμέναις, ὡς ὅταν ἐξυφήνωσι, τότε δοθησομένας πρὸς γάμον. Ἐκείνας μὲν οὖν δι' ἡμέρας ὑφαίνειν, ἑτέρας δε νύκτωρ τὸν Ταρχετίου κελεύοντος ἀναλύειν τὸν ἱστόν. Ἐκδέ τοῦ φαλλοῦ τῆς θεραπαινίδος τεκούσης δίδυμα δοῦναι τινὶ Τερατίῳ τὸν Ταρχέτιον ἀνελεῖν κελευσάντα.

SERVIUS TULLIUS.—Of whose miraculous begetting Dionysius of Halicarnassus, *Antiquitatum*, IV., 2, writes at length : Φέρεται δέ τις ἐν ταῖς ἐπιχωρίοις ἀναγραφαῖς καὶ ἕτερος ὑπὲρ τῆς γενέσεως αὐτου λόγος, ἐπὶ τὸ μυθῶδες ἐξαίρων τὰ περὶ αὐτὸν, ὃν ἐν πολλαῖς Ῥωμαϊκαῖς ἱστορίαις εὕρομεν, εἰ θεοις τε καὶ δαίμοσι λέγεσθαι φίλον, τοιοῦτός τις, ἀπὸ τῆς ἑστίαις τῶν βασιλείων, ἐφ' ἧς ἄλλας τε Ῥωμαῖοι συτελοῦσιν ἱερουργίας, καὶ τας ἀπὸ τῶν δείπνων ἀπαρχὰς ἁγίζουσιν, ὑπὲρ τοῦ πυρὸς ἀνασχειν λέγουσιν αἰδοῖον ἀνδρός. Τοῦτο δὲ θεέασθαι τὴν Ὀκρισίαν πρώτην φέρουσαν τοὺς εἰωθοτας πελάνους ἐπὶ τὸ πῦρ, καὶ αὐτίκα πρὸς τοὺς βασιλεῖς ἐλθοῦσαν εἰπεῖν, τὸν μὲν οὖν Ταρχύνιον ἀκούσαντά τε καὶ μετὰ ταῦτα ἰδόντα τὸ τέρας ἐν θαύματι γενέσθαι, τὴν δε Τανακυλίδα τὰ τ' ἄλλα σοφὴν οὖσαν καὶ δὴ καὶ τὰ μαντικὰ οὐδενὸς χεῖρον Τυρρηνῶν ἐπισταμένην εἰπεῖν πρὸς αὐτόν, ὅτι γένυς ἀπὸ τῆς ἑστίας τῆς βασιλείου πέπρωται γενέσθαι κρεῖττον ἢ κατὰ τὴν ἀνθρωπείαν φύσιν, ἐκ τῆς μιχθείσης τῷ φάσματι γυναικός. Τὰ δ' αὐτὰ καὶ τῶν ἄλλων τερατοσκόπων ἀποφηναμένων, δόξαι τῷ βασιλεῖ τὴν Ὀκρισίαν, ᾗ πρώτη ἐφάνη τὸ τέρας, εἰς ὁμιλίαν αὐτῷ συνελθεῖν καὶ μετὰ τοῦτο τὴν γυναῖκα κοσμησαμένην, οἷς ἔθος ἐστὶ κοσμεῖσθαι τὰς γαμουμένας, κατακλεισθῆναι μόνην εἰς τὸν οἶκον, ἐν ᾧ τὸ τέρας ὤφθη. Μιχθέντος δή τινος αὐτῇ θεῶν ἢ δαιμόνων, καὶ μετὰ τὴν μίξιν ἀφανισθέντος, εἴτε Ἡφαίστου, καθάπερ οἴονταί τινες, εἴτε τôυ κατ'οἰκίαν ἥρωος, ἐγκύμονα γενέσθαι καὶ τεχεῖν τοῦ Τύλλιον ἐν τôις καθήκουσι χρόνοις. PLINY, xxxvi., 27, has: "Tradunt . . . ita Seruium Tullium natum, qui regno successit. Indo et in regia cubanti puero caput arsisse uisum, creditumque Laris familiaris filium."

DIOGENES LAERTIUS.—*Plato* 11 : Σπεύσιππος δ'ἐν τῷ ἐπιγραφομένῳ Πλάτωνος περιδείπνῳ καὶ Κλέαρχος ἐν τῷ Πλάτωνος ἐγκωμίῳ καὶ Ἀναξιλαίδης ἐν τῳ δευτέρῳ περὶ φιλοσόφων φασὶν ὡς Ἀθήνησιν ἦν λόγος, ὡραίαν οὖσαν τὴν Περικτιόνην βιάζεσθαι τὸν Ἀρίστωνα καὶ μὴ ἐπιτυγχάνειν παυόμενόν τε τῆς βίας ἰδεῖν τὴν τôυ Ἀπόλλωνος ὄψιν, ὅθεν καθαρὰν γάμου φυλάξαι ἕως τῆς ἀποκνήσεως. Καὶ γίνεται Πλάτων, ὥς φησιν Ἀπολλόδωρος ἐν χρονικοῖς, ὀγδόῃ καὶ ὀγδοηκοστῇ Ὀλυμπιάδι, Θαργηλιῶνος ἑβδόμῃ· καθ'ἣν Δήλιοι τὸν Ἀπόλλωνα γενέσθαι φασί.

S. JEROME.—*Aduersus Iouinianum*, I., 42 : " Speusippus quoque sororis Platonis filius, et Clearchus in laude Platonis, et Anaxilides in secundo libro Philosophiæ, Perictionem matrem Platonis, phantasmate Apollinis oppressam ferunt, et sapientiæ principem non aliter arbitrabantur nisi de partu uirginis editum." Migne, *Patres Latini*, vol. XXIII., c. 273.

ALEXANDER THE GREAT.—Plutarch, *Alexander*, II., 2 : " Ἡ μὲν οὖν νύμφη πρὸ τῆς νυκτός, ᾗ συνείρχθησαν εἰς τὸν θάλαμον, ἔδοξε βροντῆς γενομένης ἐμπεσεῖν αὐτῆς τῇ γαστρὶ κεραυνόν, ἐκ δὲ τῆς πληγῆς πολὺ πῦρ ἀναφθέν, εἶτα ῥηγνόμενον εἰς, φλόγας πάντη φερομένας διαλυθῆναι." And also, 5 : " Ὤφθη δέ ποτε καὶ δράκων κοιμωμένης τῆς Ὀλυμπιάδος παρεκτεταμένος τῷ σώματι καὶ τοῦτο μάλιστα τοῦ Φιλίππου τὸν ἔρωτα καὶ τὰς φιλοφροσύνας ἀμαυρῶσαι λέγουσιν, ὡς μηδὲ φοιτᾶν ἔτι πολλάκις παρ' αὐτὴν ἀναπαυσόμενον, εἴτε δείσαντά τινας μαγείας ἐπ'αὐτῷ καὶ φάρμακα τῆς γυναικός, εἴτε τὴν ὁμιλίαν ὡς κρείττονι συνούσης ἀφοσιούμενον."

Quintus Curtius, IV., 7, relates that when Alexander visited the shrine of Hammon, " regem propius adeuntem maximus natu e sacerdotibus *filium* adpellat ; *hoc nomen illi parentem louem reddere* affirmans : Ille se uero ait, et accipere, et agnoscere."

SELEUCUS, King of Syria.—Justin, *Trogi Pompei Epitoma*, XV., 4, writes : " Huius [Seleuci] quoque uirtus clara et origo admirabilis fuit : siquidem mater eius Laudice, cum nupta esset Antiocho, claro inter Philippi duces uiro, uisa sibi est per quietem ex concubitu Apollinis concepisse, grauidamque factam munus concubitus a deo anulum accepisse, in cuius gemma anchora sculpta esset, iussaque donum filio quem peperisset dare. Admirabilem fecit hunc uisum et anulus, qui postera die eiusdem sculpturæ in lecto inuentus est, et figura [anchoræ] quæ in femore Seleuci nata cum ipso paruulo fuit."

Malvenda notes : Appianus scribit (in *Syriacis*) Apollinem Laodice per somnium mandasse, vt quem annulum aliquando reperisset, filio statim gestādum daret : fore namque vt quibus in orbis locis Seleucus annulum eum amisisset, eam ipse postmodum regionem Imperio suo subiiceret."

SCIPIO AFRICANUS.—" Liuius, *lib. 6, Decad.* 3, hæc inter cætera ait : Ex quo togam uirilem sumpsit, nullo die prius vllam publicam priuatamq. rem egit, quā in Capitolium iret, ingressusq. Ædem consideret, & plerumq. tempus solus in secreto ibi tereret. Hic mos qui per omnem uitam seruabatur, seu consulto, seu temere uulgatæ opinioni fidem apud quosdam fecit, stirpis eum diuinæ uirum esse, retulitq. famam in Alexandro Magno prius uulgatam, & uanitate et fabula parem : anguis immanis concubitu conceptum, & in cubiculo matris eius persæpe uisam prodigii eius speciem ; interuentuq. hominum euolutam repente, atque ex oculis elapsam."

Aulus Gellius, VII., 1, quoting from Caius Oppius and Julius Higinus, relates the same story, which says that the mother of Scipio when her husband was absent " uisum repente [esse] iuxta eam cubare ingentem anguem." Upon an alarm being raised the snake had vanished, but nine months later she bore Scipio Africanus.

CAESAR AUGUSTUS.—" In Asclepiadis Mendetis Θεολο γουμενῶν libris lego, Atiam, cum ad solenne Apollinis sacrum media nocte uenisset, posita in templo lectica, dum caeteræ matronæ dormirent, obdormisse : draconem repente irrepsisse ad cam, paulloque post egressum : illamque experge-factam quasi a concubitu mariti purificasse se : et statim in corpore eius exstitisse maculam, uelut depicti draconis : nec potuisse unquam eximi : adeo ut mox publicis balneis perpetuo abstinuerit : Augustum natum mense decimo, et ob hoc Apollinis filium existimatum." Suetonius, *Octauius Cæsar Augustus,* xciv.

ARISTOMENES THE MESSENIAN.—Strabo, *De Situ Mundi,*

VIII., 4, writing of Græcia Messenia, refers to the legend of the birth of Aristomenes.

Pausanias, IV., xiv., 7 : " Aristomenes, who is still worshipped as a hero by the Messenians. They think that even the circumstances of his birth were above the common ; for his mother Nicotelea, they say, was visited by a demon or a god in the likeness of a serpent." Translated by Sir James Frazer, vol. I., p. 200.

Pliny, XI., 37, has : " Hirto corde gigni quosdam homines proditur, neque alios fortiores esse industria, sicut Aristomenem Messenium, qui CCC occidit Lacedæmonios. Ipse conuulneratus et captus, semel per cauernam lautumiarum cuasit, angustos uulpium aditus secutus. Iterum captus, sopitis custodibus somno, ad ignem aduolutus lora cum corpore exussit. Tertio capto Lacedæmonii pectus dissicuere uiuenti, hirsutumque cor repertum est."

MERLIN.—Boece *Scotorum Historiæ*, folio 1526, VIII., says : " Constans tum fama erat, Merlinū incubi, ac nobilis Britānici sanguinis fœminæ cōcubitu, p̄gnatū, magicis carminibus malos dęmones ad colloquia excire : & ex his quę futura essent cognoscere."

There is an old romance of Merlin : *Sensuyt le p̄mier volume de Merlin. Qui est le premier liure de la Table ronde. Avec plusiers choses moult recreatiue.* P. le Noir, Paris, 1528. Here the demons, alarmed at the number of men who have escaped them since the Birth of Our Lord, hold a council of war and resolve to send to the world one of their company to engender upon some virgin a child. He shall be their vicegerent upon earth, and (*salua reuerentia*) according to their schemes endeavour to counteract the Redemption. The fiend deputed to this work obtains admittance into the house of a wealthy Briton, and true to his nature slays his host, seducing two of the three daughters. The youngest resists, but whilst in an enchanted sleep is swived by the devil. Witless of what has occurred she confesses to a holy hermit, Blaise, who protects her. She gives birth to Merlin, who is instantly baptized by Blaise, and thus the devil's designs are frustrated. Cf. James Huneker's tale *Antichrist ; Visionaries,* 1905.

One may compare Machiavelli's *Belphegor,* and the Oriental Saga of the angels Harut and Marut, in the commentators on (*Sura,* 11, 96) the Qu'ran. In the Chronicle of Philippe Moustres, Bishop of Tournai, a diabolical origin is attributed to Eleonora of Aquitaine, who espoused Louis-le-Jeune,

King of France, and afterwards was wedded to Henry II. of England. J. Brompton (*Hist. Franc.*, XIII., 215) has preserved a similar legend, and in the *Livre de Badouin* (p. 13) Comtesse Jeanne de Flandre is supposed to be a daughter of the evil spirit. See Reiffenberg, Introduction to the *Chronicle of Philippe de Moustres*, p. lxviii.

With regard to Merlin one may consult *Die Sagen von Merlin . . .* by San Marte (A. Schulz), Halle, 8vo, 1853; and *Slavianskaia Skazania o Solomonye i kitrovrase i zapadnya legendy o Morolfe i Merline*. By A. Vesselovsky, S. Petersburg, 1872.

William Rowley's *The Birth of Merlin, or the Childe hath found his Father*, not printed until 1662, and once ascribed to Shakespeare, is a curious medley of farce and romance, awkward, but not wholly destitute of poetry. Herein the Devil appears as Merlin's father. He has got Joan Go-Too't, the Clown's sister, with child, and Merlin is born amid thunder and lightning. But Merlin, rebuking his father, who dubs him " Traitor to hell ! " as

> an inferior lustful Incubus,
> Taking advantage of the wanton Flesh,

encloses him in a rock, and conveys his mother to a secure retreat.

Malvenda's authority is the *Chronica* of John Nauclerus, volumen secundum, generatio xv. " Inuentus est tum adolescens dictus Merlinus, cuius mater confessa est se a spiritu in specie hominis concepisse, hoc est, per incubum. hic Merlinus Ambrosius est dictus natus ex filia regis Demetæ, quæ monada erat." The marginal note has " Merlinus ab incubo dæmone conceptus," p. 559, folio, Cologne, 1579.

MARTIN LUTHER.—The story of Luther's alleged generation is related by Malvenda in c. VI. of his *De Antichristo* with title, *Martinus Lutherus creditus a quibusdam uerus Antichristus*.

" Ex incubo dæmonio genitum haud leuibus futilibusque coniecturis deprehensum est a plerisque, vt Coclæus refert " (p. 71). See the *Historia Ioannis Cochlæi de Actis et Scriptis Martini Lutheri*, Paris, 1565.

Johann Cochlæus, properly Dobeneck, and named Cochlæus from his native place, Wendelstein, near Schwabach, was born 1479; and died 11 January, 1552, at Breslau. After a brilliant career as a student and professor of theology, he was ordained at Rome in 1518, and was shortly to make his mark

as an active opponent of the Lutheran movement. With
indomitable ardour he poured forth pamphlet after pamphlet,
and although it is hardly to be expected that everything from
his pen has the same value, the bulk of his work is an excellent
refutation of the contemporary anarchy and looseness of
thought. His editions of ecclesiastical writers, and such
historical studies as *Historiæ Hussitarum*, XII. *Libri* (1549),
are of permanent value, as also is his sound criticism of Luther
and the new tenets.

P. 23. BENEDICT PEREIRA.—Benedict Pereira, born
about 1535 at Ruzafa, near Valencia ; died 6 March, 1610, at
Rome. He entered the Society of Jesus in 1552, and became
famous in Rome for his lectures on scripture. His works
are exceptionally lengthy and full. The main difficulties of
Genesis are discussed and solved in his *Commentariorum et
Disputationum in Genesim tomi quattuor*, Rome, 1591–99.

P. 24. MICHAEL ETTMÜLLER.—This famous German
doctor was born at Leipzig, 10 May, 1644, and died 9 March,
1683. He was Professor of Botany, Surgery, and Anatomy
at Leipzig, and won universal renown. A compendium of
his many medical writings, *Opera omnia in compendium redacta*,
was published at London, 8vo, in 1701. He left a son,
Ernest Michael Ettmüller (ob. 1732), who although not so
distinguished yet honourably carried on the family tradition.

P. 25. MAGNUS ALEXANDER.—This pretty pentameter,
which is universally quoted as "an old saw" does not appear
to have been traced to its original.

P. 26. CORNELIUS À LAPIDE.—Cornelis Cornelissen Van
Der Steen (Cornelius Cornelii à Lapide), Flemish Jesuit and
exegete, was born at Bocholt, 18 December, 1567 ; died at
Rome 12 March, 1637. He wrote very ample commentaries
upon Holy Scripture, with the exception of Job and the
Psalms. His works have been reprinted again and again,
translated into many languages, and are continually referred
to by Biblical writers. I have used the Antwerp edition,
folio, 1659, of the *Commentaria in Pentateuchum Mosis*, Cap.
VI. (p. 107); upon the words *Gigantes autem erant* the gloss
runs : "Burgensis putat gigantes fuisse dæmones, humana
specie indutos : Ualesius putat gigantes fuisse filios dæmonum
incuborum : Philo putat homines sceleratissimos uocari
gigantes. Sed certum est gigantes fuisse homines monstruosa
statura robore, latrociniis, & tyrannide insignes, vnde
gigãtes, per sua scelera, fuerunt maxima & potissima causa

diluuii, vt patet Sap. 14, u 6, Iob 26.5. Idem insinuat hic Moses : ea enim de causa descripturus diluuium, gigantes, quasi diluuii causam, præmittit, ita passim docent interpretes." *Wisdom*, XIV., 6 : "And from the beginning also when the proud giants perished, the hope of the world fleeing to a vessel, which was governed by thy hand, left to the world seed of generation." *Job* xxvi., 5 : "Behold the giants groan under the waters, and they that dwell with them."

BURGENSIS.—Paul de Santa Maria, a Spanish Archbishop, Lord Chancellor, and exegete, born at Burgos about 1351 ; died 29 August, 1435. The most wealthy and influential Jew of Burgos (Jewish name Solomon-Ha-Levi), and a scholar of the first rank in Talmudic and Rabbinical literature, a Rabbi of the Hebraic community, he was converted to Christianity by the irrefutable logic of the *Summa* of S. Thomas. He received baptism 21 July, 1390. His reputation as a Biblical writer chiefly rests upon his *Additiones* to the *Postilla* of Nicholas of Lyra, Nuremburg, 1481 ; Venice, 1481 ; and many other editions.

P. 27. CELSUS.—Juventius Celsus, two Roman Jurists, father and son, both of whom are quoted in the *Digest*. Very little is known of the elder Celsus. The younger Celsus, who was the more celebrated, lived under Nerva and Trajan, by whom he was highly favoured. He wrote *Digesta* in thirty-nine books, *Epistolæ*, *Quæstiones* and *Institutiones* in seven books. See Pliny, *Epistles*, VI., 5.

P. 28. INNOCENT III.—Born 1160 or 1161 ; died 1216. One of his greatest acts was the convocation of the Fourth Lateran Council, which he solemnly opened 15 November, 1215.

P. 28. DOMINGO BAÑEZ.—More properly Vañez. A famous Dominican theologian, born 1528, died 1604. He has been described as a figure of unprecedented distinction in scholastic Spain. Fidelity to S. Thomas was his strongest characteristic. "Never," he was wont to say, "never by so much as a finger-nail's breadth even in lesser things, have I ever departed from the teaching of S. Thomas."

SISTO OF SIENA.—Dominican theologian and demonologist. His chief work is *Bibliotheca Sancta*, Libri V., Francofurti, folio, 1575 (secunda editio).

PICO DELLA MIRANDOLA.—The famous Italian philosopher and scholar, 1463-1494.

P. 28. MOLINA.—Luis de Molina, S.J., one of the most learned and most renowned theologians of the Society of Jesus, was born at Cuenca 1535, and died at Madrid 1600. Professor of theology in the flourishing University of Evora, for twenty years he lectured upon the *Summa* of S. Thomas to thronging audiences. The results of this profound study of thirty years he published as *Concordia liberi arbitrii cum gratiæ donis, diuina præscientia, prouidentia, prædestinatione et reprobatione*, Lisbon, 1588. The work, which is primarily concerned with reconciling grace and free will, caused endless discussion and controversy. Molina's *Commentaria in primam partem D. Thomae* (2 vols.) was printed at Cuenca in 1592.

P. 28. BARTOLOMÉ CARRANZA.—Dominican Archbishop of Toledo, born 1503 ; died 1576. He was present at the Council of Trent, but owing (it would seem) to malice and misrepresentation he fell under suspicion of unorthodoxy, and the Grand Inquisitor Valdes brought an action against him. The suit dragged on wearily and ended unsatisfactorily. The Archbishop was found not guilty of heresy, but he had rendered himself suspect of certain propositions tinged with Lutheranism.

P. 28. BONAVENTURA BARON.—A distinguished Irish Franciscan theologian, philosopher, and writer of Latin prose and verse, born at Clonmel, County Tipperary, 1610, and died at Rome 18 March, 1696. He especially devoted himself to a defence of the Scotist philosophy, and his *Scotus defensus et amplificatus* (3 vols.), Cologne, 1664, is a work of highest merit. He was appointed historiographer (1676) to Cosmo de' Medici, Grand-duke of Tuscany, and was elected a member of the Florentine Academy. His writings are both elegant, learned, and correct.

P. 30. CIENFUEGOS.—Cardinal Francisco Javier de Cienfuegos y Jovellanos, S.J., a famous theologian, is especially known for his writings on the Mass. He was given the Red Hat by Clement XI.

P. 42. NICOLAS LÉMERY.—The celebrated French chemist, was born at Rouen, 17 November, 1645, and died at Paris 19 June, 1715. He published his *Cours de Chimie, contenant la manière de faire les opérations qui sont en usage dans la médecine par une methode facile avec des raisonnements sur chaque opération, pour l'instruction de ceux qui veulent s'appliquer à cette science*, at Paris, 8vo, 1675. The work had an amazing success, and when Lémery was in England, 1683, he presented the fifth edition to King Charles II. It has been re-issued no less than thirty-one times. The best edition is generally considered to be that of Baron, 4to, 1756.

P. 43. CROWS, STAGS, RAVENS.—*Pliny, Historia Naturalis,* VII., xlix., 48 : " De spatio atque longinquitate uitæ hominum, non locorum modo situs, uerum exempla, ac sua cuique sors nascendi incertum fecere. Hesiodus, qui primus aliqua de hoc prodidit, fabulose (ut reor) multa de hominum aeuo referens, cornici nouem nostras attribuit aetates, quadruplum eius ceruis, id triplicatum coruis. Et reliqua fabulosius in phœnice, ac Nymphis." Pliny often repeats these tales of the old age of these animals. Many authors write thus of the crow, *e.g.,* Lucretius, *De Natura Rerum,* V., 1083 :

> et partim mutant cum tempestatibus una
> raucisonos cantus, cornicum ut sæcla uetusta
> coruorumque greges ubi aquam dicuntur et imbris
> poscere et interdum uentos aurasque uocare.

Horace, *Carminum,* III., xvii., 13 : aquæ nisi fallit augur, Annosa cornix. Ovid, *Metamorphoseon,* VII., 274 : Ora caputque nouem cornicis sæcula passæ. Aratus has : εννιάχηρα κορώνη. Cicero, *Tusculanarum,* III., xxviii., 69, writes : " Theophrastus autem moriens accusasse naturam dicitur, quod ceruis et cornicibus uitam diuturnam, quorum id nihil interesset ; hominibus, quorum maxime interfuisset, tam exiguam uitam dedisset."

TACITUS.—*Annals,* VI., 28 : " Paullo Fabio L. Uitellio Coss. post longum sæculorum ambitum auis Phœnix in Ægyptum uenit. . . . De numero annorum uaria traduntur. Maxime uulgatum quingentorum spatium. Sunt qui adseuerent, mille quadringentos sexaginta unum interiici ; prioresque alites Sesostride primum, post Amaside dominantibus, dein Ptolemæo, qui ex Macedonibus tertius regnauit. . . . aduolauisse. Sed antiquitas quidem obscura. . . . Haec incerta et fabulosis aucta."

P. 44. S. AUGUSTINE.—*De Diuinatione dæmonum,* written 406–411. Migne, XL., 581–592.

P. 46. GODFREY OF FONTAINES.—*Doctor Uenerandus,* born near Liège in the first half of the thirteenth century ; a Canon of Liège, Paris, and Cologne. He was elected in 1300 to the see of Tournai, but refused the episcopate. During the last quarter of the century he taught theology at the University of Paris. He is the author of a most notable collection of disputations. *XIV. Quodlibeta.* A modern critical edition of these has been prepared by de Wulf.

P. 51. PELTANUS.—Theodore Peltanus, a Biblical scholar of note, who translated several commentaries from Greek into Latin. His glosses are valuable. His translation of the *Commentary on the Apocalypse* by Bishop Andrew of Cæsarea was published 4to, 1584.

Andrew of Cæsarea, Cappodocia, is assigned by Krumbacher to the first half of the sixth century, although by others he is variously placed from the fifth to the ninth century. His *Commentary on the Apocalypse* is important as the first exegesis of that book we know, the source whence most writers have largely drawn. The original has been printed by Migne, *Patres Graeci,* CVI., 215–458, 1387–94. See Krumbacher, *Gesch. der byzant. Lit.* (pp. 129–131), 2nd edition, Munich, 1897.

P. 51. PETER THYRAEUS.—Peter Thyracus, S.J., Doctor of Theology, the younger brother of the more famous Hermann Thyraeus, S.J., Jesuit provincial of the Rhine (born 1532 ; *ob.* 1591). Peter Thyraeus was born at Neuss on the Rhine, and owing to his learning occupied several important positions in that province. I have used the Rind edition of the *De Terrificationibus Nocturnis. Dæmoniaci cum Locis Infestis et Terriculamentis Nocturnis,* auctore Petro Thyraeo Neuesiano, Societatis Iesu, Doctore Theologo. Coloniæ Agrippinæ, 8vo, 1604. Caput II. (p. 332), has as rubric : *Docetur Terrificationes, & dictos Tumultus non fieri ab Homuncionibus quibusdam : sed nec esse Tales, quales dicuntur, Homunciones.* The author decides that Spirits and Ghosts are the causes of these midnight noises and fears.

P. 53. ARISTOTLE.—The work known as the *Problems* is, of course, wrongly attributed to the great Greek philosopher. The earliest edition was printed in 1475 at Rome. There are translations into nearly all modern languages. In 1710 was published in London the twenty-fifth English edition. The book is frequently reprinted, and common even to-day.

The *De Uirtute Herbarum* is no longer considered to be the work of Apuleius.

P. 53. GERMANDER.—The name of the plants of the genus *Teuerium.* Harrison, *England,* II., xx., 1587 (ed. 1877 ; I., 326) has : " Our common germander or thistle benet is . . . of . . . great power in medicine." A. T. Thomson, *London Dispensary,* 1811 (ed. 1818 ; p. 398) writes : " Wall

Germander [Teuerium Chamædrys] has been accounted tonic, stomachic, [etc.]."

Palma Christi, the castor oil plant. *Ricinus communis.* Turner, *Names of Herbs*, 1548, notes : " Ricinus is called ... in English Palma Christi." Even to-day almost miraculous effects are attributed to this plant by the native superstitions of the West Indies.

P. 56. SWEET CALAMUS.—*Calamus aromaticus*, an Eastern aromatic plant, said to be the sweet-scented Lemon Grass of Malabar, *Andropogon Schœnanthus*, Jeremias, vi., 20, the Vulgate has : Ut quid mihi thus de Saba affertis, et *calamum suaue olentem* de terra longinqua ? The Douay Bible translates : " the sweet smelling cane " ; Coverdale (1535) : " Sweete smellinge Calamus." A.V. : " the sweet cane," so R.V. with marginal note " Or, *calamus.*" Some English herbalists have applied the name *calamus aromaticus* to the native Sweet Flag, or Sweet Rush (*Acorus calamus*).

Cubeb seed.—The berry of a climbing shrub, *Piper Cubeba* or *Cubeba officinalis*, a native of Java and the adjacent isles. It resembles a grain of pepper, and had a pungent spicy flavour. It is used in medicine and cookery.

Aristolochies.—Aristolochia, a genus of shrubs, one of which, the Common Birthwort, is found in Britain. Topsell, *Four-footed Beasts* (1607), speaks of : " Aristoloch, otherwise called Hartwort."

Cardamom.—A spice used in medicine as a stomachic, and also for flavouring sauces and curries. The only kind in the British pharmacopœia is the Malabar cardamom obtained from *E. Cardamomum.*

Long-Pepper.—A condiment prepared from the immature fruit-spikes of the allied plants *Piper (Chavica) officinarum* and *Piper longum (C. Roxbrughii).* It was formerly supposed to be the flower or unripe fruit of *Piper nigrum.* Harley, *Materia Medica* (Sixth edition, 1876), p. 434, tells us : " Long Pepper has been employed by the Hindoos in medicine from the earliest times."

Caryophylleæ.—Greek, καρυόφυλλον = the clove pink.

Calamite Storax.—Pechey, *Compleat Herbalist* (1694), 333, has : " The resin of storax, which is sold in the shops is two-fold, dry and liquid. The dry is called Storax Calamite ... because it is put up in Reeds."

P. 57. CARTHUSIAN FRIARY.—The famous Certosa di Pavia, founded in 1396 by Gian Galeazzo Visconti.

P. 58. EXSURGAT DEUS.—Psalm lxvii. *Qui habitat,* Psalm xc.

P. 59. AGRIMONY.—*Agrimonia Eupatorica.* Or liver-wort, of the genus *hepatica,* applied to plants used in diseases of the liver, or having liver-shaped parts.

Spurge.—One or other of several species of plants belonging to the very extensive genus *Euphorbia,* many of which are characterised by an acrid milky juice, possessing purgative and medicinal properties.

P. 60. CALLIONYMUS.—The Vulgate has : Ecce piscis immanis exiuit ad deuorandum eum [Tobiam]. *Liber Tobiæ,* VI., 2. Callionymus = καλλιώνυμος, *i.e.,* with beautiful name, by which term Hipparchus mentions the fish *uranoscopus scaber.* Pliny, *Historia Naturalis,* XXXII., 7, writes : " Callionymi fel cicatrices sanat, et carnes oculorum superuacuas consumit. Nulli hoc piscium copiosius, ut existimauit Menander quoque in comœdiis. Idem piscis et uranoscopos uocatur, ab oculo quem in capite habet." Gabriel Brotier in his notes upon Pliny, Barbou edition, Paris, 1779, tom. V., p. 467, translates callionymus by "le Tapeçon."

P. 62. PLINY.—*Historia Naturalis,* XXXII., 7 : "Omnium piscium fluuiatilium marinorumque adeps liquefactus sole admixto melle, oculorum claritati plurimum confert : item castoreum cum melle. Callionymi fel cicatrices sanat, et carnes oculorum superuacuas consumit."

P. 63. ASMODEUS.—τὸ πονηρὸν δαιμόνιον. A demon identified by some rabbis with Samaël. He is also called Chammadaï and Sydonaï. A few commentators even hold that he is the same as Beelzebub or Apollyon (*Apocalypse,* ix. 2), an extremely unlikely view. Johan Weyer, however, in his *Pseudo-monarchia dæmonum* appended to the 1577 edition of *De præstigiis dæmonum,* gives some fantastic details concerning him. It has been suggested that Asmodeus is perhaps the Persian *Aēshma daêva,* who in the *Avesta* is next to Angromainyus, the chief of evil spirits. But the name Asmodeus may be Semitic. The Aramaic word *'áshmeday* is cognate with the Hebrew *hashmed,* "destruction." Talmudic legend says that Asmodeus, or Asmodai, was implicated in the drunkenness of Noe, and has some truly extravagant tales concerning him and King Solomon. Moreover, Asmodeus is regarded as the counterpart of Lilith, and sometimes described as a jocular elf. (*Cf.* Le Sage's *Le Diable Boiteux.*) Wünsche ; *Der bab. Talm.* II., 180–3. Asmodeus was one of the devils who possessed Madeleine Bavent of the convent of SS. Louis and Elizabeth at Louvias in 1642–43.

P. 64. S. JEROME.—The famous *Uita Pauli* was written 374–9. It may be found in Migne, XXIII., 17–28, and there is a separate edition by Tamietti, Turin, 1903.

P. 64. S. PAUL. A.D. 341.—S. Paul, who dwelt in the Lower Thebaid, died on 10 January, on which day he is commemorated in most ancient Martyrologies. But both Latins and Greeks have transferred his festival to 15 January so as to fall outside the closed Octave of the Epiphany. There are fine pictures of the meeting of S. Paul and S. Antony by Pintu ricchio, Lucas van Leyden, Velasquez, and Guido. Brusasorci in a magnificent canvas shows us the Centaur and the Satyr, two diminutive figures in the background of the landscape where the solitaries are communing.

P. 64. S. ANTONY.—S. Antony the Great, father of monks, born about 251. His feast is celebrated in all kalendars, 17 January. The passage quoted by Sinistrari occurs in the Sixth Lection of the Second Nocturn at Matins.

P. 69. GEORGE AGRICOLA.—Georg Landmann, the celebrated German metallurgist, was born at Chemnitz, Saxony, 24 March, 1494, and died here in 1555. His chief work is the *De re Metallica*, Bâle, 4to, 1546. The *De Animantibus subterraneis* was published at Bâle, folio, 1657, with other of his treatises. The passage to which Sinistrari refers may be read upon p. 491 : "Postremo in subterraneam animantium, seu, quod placet theologis, substantiam numero haberi possunt dæmones, qui in quibusdam uersantur fodinis. Eorum autem duplex est genus. Sunt enim truculenti & terribiles aspectu, qui plerunq ; metallicis infesti atq ; inimici sunt. . . . Sunt deinde mites, quos Germanorum alii, ut etiam Græci, uocant Cobalos [Kobolts] quod hominum sunt imitatores. Nam quasi lætitia gestientes rident, & multa uidentur facere, quum prorsus nihil faciant. Alii nominant uirunculos montanos . . . uidentur autem esse seneciones & uestiti more metallicorum. . . . Quanquam uero interdum glareis lacessunt operarios, rarissime tamen eos laedunt. Nec laedunt unquam nisi prius ipsi cachinno fuerint, aut maledicto lacessiti. . . . Sed dæmones montani potissimum laborant in his specubus e quibus metalla effodiuntur iam, uel ea effodi posse spes est. Quodcirca metallici non deterentur a laboribus, sed omnem inde capientes alacriori animo sunt & uehementius laborant."

P. 70.   S. AUGUSTINE.—The *De Genesi* was written 401–15;
Migne, xxxiv., 245–486.   The *Enarrationes in Psalmos*, composed in 415, will be found apud Migne, xxxvi., 66–1906.

P. 72.   LYRA.—Nicholas of Lyra, Doctor planus et utilis,
Franciscan, 1270–1340.   His greatest work is the monumental
Postillæ perpetuæ in uniuersam S. Scripturam, which was the
first commentary on the Bible actually to be printed.

Francis Titelmann, Capuchin, Professor of Exegesis in the
University of Louvain, whence he retired in 1536 wholly to
devote himself to the religious life.   He won a European
reputation by his controversy with Erasmus, and has written
very profound commentaries on the Scriptures.

Gilbert Génebrard, O.S.B., exegete and Oriental scholar,
Archbishop of Aix, 1535–97.   He was one of the most learned
professors of the day, and his works were regarded as
authoritative throughout Europe.   One of the best known
of these is his *Psalmi Dauidis uulgata editione, calendario hebræo,
syro, græco, latino, hymnis, argumentis, et commentariis, etc.,
instructi* (Paris, 1577).

P. 72.   HUGH OF ST-CHER, a Dominican Cardinal of the
thirteenth century ; born about 1200, died in 1263.   He is the
author of many works on Holy Scripture, and is justly regarded
as the first compiler of a Biblical Concordance, the model
for all subsequent publications of this kind.

P. 76.   FRANCISCO TOLEDO.—Philosopher, theologian,
and exegete, born at Cordova, 1532 ; died at Rome, 1596.
He entered the Society of Jesus, 1558, and was professor at
Rome, 1564 ; 17 September, 1593, he was created a Cardinal
by Pope Clement VIII.   By many scholars his Scriptural
Commentaries were considered the clearest and most concise
of the day.   He was a prolific writer, and his works have run
into numerous editions.   Gregory XIII. esteemed him as a
pillar of learning, whilst Soto ranks him as a genius.

P. 77.   BALAAM.—*Numbers*, xxiv., especially v.   17 :
Orietur Stella ex Iacob, et consurget Uirga de Israel.

P. 77.   MERCURIUS TRISMEGISTUS.—Hermes Trismegistus,
the supposed author of a large number of works, many of
which are still extant.   As early as the time of Plato the Greek
god Hermes was identified with the Egyptian Thoth.   The
Neo-Platonists regarded an Egyptian Hermes as the source of
all intellectual knowledge, in fact, the Logos incarnate.   It was
pretended that from him Pythagoras and Plato had derived
their wisdom.   A large number of mystical and occult works

were ascribed to this Hermes. Most of these writings belong to the fourth century of our era. Lactantius *De Falsa Religione*, I., 7, writes : " Quid, quod Mercurius ille ter maximus ; cujus supra mentionem feci ; non modo ἀμήτωρα, ut Apollo, sed ἀπάτωρα, quoque appellat Deum ; quod origo illi non sit aliunde ? Nec enim potest ab ullo esse generatus, qui ipse uniuersa generauerit. Satis (ut opinor) & argumentis docui, et testibus confirmaui, quod per se satis clarum est, Unum esse regem mundi, unum patrem, unum Deum."

Hydaspes, or Hystaspes, is said to have been an ancient King of the Medes from whom is derived the name of the river Hydaspes. (*Medus Hydaspes*, Vergil, Georgics, IV., 211 ; *fabulosus Hydaspes*, Horace, Odes I., xxii., 7.) Clement of *Alexandria, Stromata*, VI., says : " Librosque Græcos sumite, agnoscite Sibyllam, quomodo unum Deum significet, et ea quæ sunt futura, et Hystaspen sumite et legite, et inuenietis Dei filium multo clarius et apertius esse scriptum, et quemadmodum aduersus Christum multi reges instituent aciem, qui eum habent odio, et eos qui nomen eius gestant, et eius fideles, et eius tolerantiam et aduentem." Other authors who mention King Hydaspes are Agathias in Book II. of his *History;* Ammianus Marcellinus, Book XXIII. ; S. Justin Martyr in his *Apology*, II. ; and Theodore Canterus, c. 19. Lactantius, *De Uita Beata*, VII., 15, writes : " Hystaspes quoque, qui fuit Medorum rex antiquissimus, a quo amnis quoque nomen accepit, qui nunc Hydaspes dicitur, admirabile somnium, sub interpretatione uaticinantis pueri ad memoriam posteris tradidit, sublatum iri ex orbe imperium, nomenque Romanum ; multo ante præfatus, quam illa Troiana gens conderetur."

P. 77. THE SYBILS.—Lactantius, Book I., *De Falsa Religione*, discusses these prophetic women at great length, and in his *De Uera Sapientia*, IV., 6, he distinctly says, that Christ " summi Dei filium . . . non tantum congruentes in unum uoces prophetarum, sed etiam Trismegisti prædicatio, et Sibyllarum uaticinia demonstrant." He then discusses the oracle delivered by the Erythræan Sibyl.

P. 77. BARONIUS.—The Venerable Cesare Baronius, Oratorian, Cardinal, and ecclesiastical historian, 1538–1607. His *Annals*, the first volume of which appeared in 1588, have earned for him the title of Father of Ecclesiastical History.

P. 78. FULGENTIUS.—Saint Fabius Claudius Gordianus Fulgentius ; born 468, died 533 ; Bishop of Ruspe, N. Africa, is eminent among the Fathers of the Church for his sanctity, eloquence, writings, and theological learning. His sermons, if few in number, are eloquent and full of fervour. His works may be found in Migne, *Patres Latini*, LXV.

P. 78. MARIA DE AGREDA.—Maria Coronel, or, as she is more commonly known, Maria de Agreda, from the little town in Old Castile where she was born in 1602, was a discalced Franciscan nun. She entered her convent in January, 1619, and when only twenty-five years old, by Papal dispensation, she was made Abbess. With the exception of an interval of three years she remained Superior until her death 24 May, 1665. The convent under her administration became one of the most fervent in Spain. She had the greatest influence over King Philip IV., whom she advised excellently and with complete common sense. Her letters to the King have been printed. She died with the reputation of a saint, and the cause of her canonization was introduced before the Congregation of Rites 21 June, 1672. She has become famous by her great work, *La mistica ciudad de Dios, historia divina de la Virgen, Madre de Dios*. It was printed in Madrid in 1670. *The Mystical City* is a series of most profound revelations concerning the life of Our Lady. It met with extraordinary opposition, and, upon false information, was even censured at Rome. This sublime work, however, is sanctioned and praised in a Bull of Benedict XIV., 16 January, 1748. *La Mistica Ciudad de Dios* has been translated into French, 2nd edition, 6 vols., 1862. Chapters XXII.–XXX. contain account of the flight into Egypt, of the sojourn of Our Lady there, the miracles She worked, and how She converted many of the Egyptians.

P. 79. NICEPHORUS.—Callistus Xanthopulus Nicephorus, the author of an Ecclesiastical History, was born in the latter part of the thirteenth century and died about 1350. His work has been edited by Duchène, Paris, 1630, 2 vols., folio.

SUIDAS, the Greek lexicographer, who probably lived in either the tenth or eleventh century. The lexicon is a dictionary of words arranged in alphabetical order, but it is not well conceived, since some articles are ample and others very scanty. There are several editions, especially those by Gaisford, Oxford, 1834; and by Bekker, 1854.

CEDRENUS.—Georgius Cedrenus, a Byzantine writer, author of an historical work, which begins with the creation of the world and goes down to A.D. 1057. Edited by Bekker, Bonn, 1838–39.

P. 79. COMMENTARY UPON AGGÆUS, II. 8.—Et mouebo
omnes Gentes. Cornelius à Lapide writes at great length
upon this verse. " Primo per bella ciuilia, . . . Ita Mariana.
Secundò, in censu quo omnes profecti ad suas ciuitates, coge-
bantur profiteri se Augusto esse subiectos. Tertio, per præ-
dicationem and miracula Christi & Apostolorum, perque
portenta edita in cælo & in terra, tam nascente, quam
patiente Christo, quæ iam recensui, commotæ sunt Gentes
ad pœnitentiam, & ad fidem Christi capessendam." See
Cornelius à Lapide, *Commentaria in Aggæum Prophetam*, Cap.
II. v. 8. apud *Commentaria in Duodecim Prophetas Minores*,
Antwerp, folio, 1720, pp. 615–20.

P. 80. ECHINADES.—Small islands at the mouth of the river
Achelous, the largest river in Greece, Aspro Potamo. This
river rises in Mount Pindus and falls into the Ionian Sea.
The largest island, Dulichium, is at present united to the
mainland.

P. 84. S. BERNARD.—S. Bernard of Clairvaux, 1090–1153.
There are three early lives of this Saint, and his acts have
been fully treated by the Bollandists.

P. 84. S. PETER OF ALCANTARA, Franciscan of the Strict
Observance, 1499–1562. His Feast is celebrated 19 October.
There are several lives of the Saint and in particular that by
Paulo, *Uita S. Petri*, Rome, 1669, may be noticed. See also
the *Acta Sanctorum*, October, VIII, 636 *sqq.*

P. 86. VENUS AS BORN OF THE SEA.—Aphrodite sprang
from the foam of the sea into which was thrown the mutilated
body of Uranus. See Hesiod, *Theogony*, 180–209, also Apollo-
dorus the Grammarian, *Bibliotheca*, I., 1 ; Servius on the
Aeneid, V., 801 ; and *Eclogues*, VI., 18. Also Tibullus, I., ii.,
39–40 :—

> Nam fuerit quicunque loquax, is sanguine natam,
> Is Uenerem e rapido sentiet esse mari.

P. 95. INTRICATE KNOTS.—*La Ghirlanda delle Streghe*, a
long cord tied in elaborate knots with the feathers of a black
hen inserted in the strands. This is hidden away in some
secret place with appropriate maledictions, and the person at
whom the bane is launched will be consumed with a swift
disease no doctor can cure. Strangely enough one of these
enchanted ropes was in 1886 found in the belfry of an English
country church. All were puzzled, for it was evidently
twined and twisted for some specific purpose. An old woman

in the village identified it as a " witch's ladder," but it was not until an engraving had been published in *The Folk Lore Journal* that full information was received and the purport of the mysterious charm completely understood.

P. 95. TOADS.—When the North Berwick coven of witches, 1590, attempted the life of King James, Agnes Sampson pressed the Devil to destroy His Highness without delay. " The Deuill ansuerit, he sould do quhat he could, bott it wald be lang to, because it wald be thoirterit [thwarted], and he promeist to hir and thame ane pictour of walx, and ordenit hir and thame to hing, roist, and drop one taid, and to lay the droppis of the toad [mixed with other foulness and venom] in his hienes way, quhair his Maiestie wald gang inowre or outowre, or in ony passage quhair itt mycht drop vpoun his heines heid or body, for his hienes distructioune, that ane vther mycht haif rewlit in his Maiesties place." The magic use of wax figures passed from ancient Egypt to Greece and Rome. About the end of the seventh century the life of King Duffus of Scotland was attempted in this way, see G. K. Sharp's *Witchcraft in Scotland*, 1884, p. 21. The wax image appears again and again in the witch-trials throughout the centuries. In 1664 the chief indictment against Christian Green and Margaret Agar of Brewham, Somerset, was that they had made " pictures " of wax into which they stuck thorns and needles, whereby those whose figures the models were languished and died. Glanvill, *Saducismus Triumphatus*, 1681, Part II, pp. 147–167. The " oil or viscid ointments " were " flying ointments " three formulæ for which have been preserved. In 1324 Dame Alice Kyteler of Kilkenny and a whole coven of witches were indicted by the Bishop of Ossory upon multiplied charges of sorcery. " In rifling the closet of the ladie, they found a wafer of sacramental bread, having the divels name stamped thereon in steed of Jesus Christ, and a pipe of ointment, wherewith she greased a staffe, upon which she ambled and gallopped through thicke and thin, when and in what manner she would." See my *Geography of Witchcraft*, pp. 85–91. Lambert Daneau, *Les Sorciers*, 1574 (English translation by Z. Jones *A Dialogue of Witches*, 1575), speaking of witches going to the sabbat says : " He [the devil] promisett that himself will conuay them thither, that are so weak that they cannot trauaile of themselues : which many tymes he doth by meanes of a staffe or rod, which he deliuereth vnto thē, or promiseth to doo it by force of a certen oynment, which he will geue them : and sometimes he offreth them an horse to ride vpon." Boguet, also, describing the journey to the sabbat, notes that some of the witches " encor se frottent auparauant de certaine graisse, & oignement."

P. 96. CERTAIN NOISE.—Poppysma. Ut explicat Pierre-Emmanuel Pierruges, *Glossarium Eroticum*, Parisiis, 1826 : " Oris pressi sonus, similis illi quo permulcentur equi et canes. Obscene uero de susurro cunni laborium, quum frictu madescunt." Uerbum est Græcum ποππυζεῖν. Auctor autem inuenit hoc uocabulum apud Martialem, VII., 18, *In Gallam*.

Quum tibi sit facies, de qua nec femina possit
Dicere ; quum corpus litura nulla notet ;
Cur te tam rarus cupiat, repetatque fututor,
Miraris ? Uitium est non leue, Galla, tibi.
Accessi quoties ad opus, mixtisque mouemur
Inguinibus ; cunnus non tacet, ipsa taces.
Di facerent, ut tu loquereris, et ipse taceret !
Offendor cunni garrulitate tui.
Pedere te mallem : namque hoc nec inutile dicit
Symmachus, et risum res mouet ista simul.
Quis ridere potest fatui poppysmata cunni ?
Quum sonat hic, cui non mentula mensque cadit ?
Dic aliquid saltem, clamosoque obstrepe cunno :
Et si adeo muta es, disce uel inde loqui.

Politian in his *Liber Miscellaneorum*, c. xxxii., discusses the word *poppysma*. A note upon this passage in Martial (ed. Lemaire, Paris, 1825, II., p. 212) says : " Poppysmata. Uox fictitia, a sono quo equis necdum domitis blandimur." Beau in his commentary upon Martial notes : " Les médecins appellent ces poppysmata une sonoréité vaginale et disent que la Galla dont il est question dans cette épigramme de Martial, était atteinte de pneumatose."

P. 96. THE DISCREETS.—In a convent of Poor Clares the Superiors under the abbess are the Vicaress, Novice Mistress, two Porteresses, and eight Discreets forming the Council. The officers are elected by the sisters in Chapter.

A CATALOG OF SELECTED
DOVER BOOKS
IN ALL FIELDS OF INTEREST

A CATALOG OF SELECTED DOVER BOOKS IN ALL FIELDS OF INTEREST

DRAWINGS OF REMBRANDT, edited by Seymour Slive. Updated Lippmann, Hofstede de Groot edition, with definitive scholarly apparatus. All portraits, biblical sketches, landscapes, nudes. Oriental figures, classical studies, together with selection of work by followers. 550 illustrations. Total of 630pp. 9⅛ × 12¼.
21485-0, 21486-9 Pa., Two-vol. set $25.00

GHOST AND HORROR STORIES OF AMBROSE BIERCE, Ambrose Bierce. 24 tales vividly imagined, strangely prophetic, and decades ahead of their time in technical skill: "The Damned Thing," "An Inhabitant of Carcosa," "The Eyes of the Panther," "Moxon's Master," and 20 more. 199pp. 5⅜ × 8½. 20767-6 Pa. $3.95

ETHICAL WRITINGS OF MAIMONIDES, Maimonides. Most significant ethical works of great medieval sage, newly translated for utmost precision, readability. Laws Concerning Character Traits, Eight Chapters, more. 192pp. 5⅜ × 8½.
24522-5 Pa. $4.50

THE EXPLORATION OF THE COLORADO RIVER AND ITS CANYONS, J. W. Powell. Full text of Powell's 1,000-mile expedition down the fabled Colorado in 1869. Superb account of terrain, geology, vegetation, Indians, famine, mutiny, treacherous rapids, mighty canyons, during exploration of last unknown part of continental U.S. 400pp. 5⅜ × 8½. 20094-9 Pa. $6.95

HISTORY OF PHILOSOPHY, Julián Marías. Clearest one-volume history on the market. Every major philosopher and dozens of others, to Existentialism and later. 505pp. 5⅜ × 8½. 21739-6 Pa. $8.50

ALL ABOUT LIGHTNING, Martin A. Uman. Highly readable non-technical survey of nature and causes of lightning, thunderstorms, ball lightning, St. Elmo's Fire, much more. Illustrated. 192pp. 5⅜ × 8½. 25237-X Pa. $5.95

SAILING ALONE AROUND THE WORLD, Captain Joshua Slocum. First man to sail around the world, alone, in small boat. One of great feats of seamanship told in delightful manner. 67 illustrations. 294pp. 5⅜ × 8½. 20326-3 Pa. $4.95

LETTERS AND NOTES ON THE MANNERS, CUSTOMS AND CONDITIONS OF THE NORTH AMERICAN INDIANS, George Catlin. Classic account of life among Plains Indians: ceremonies, hunt, warfare, etc. 312 plates. 572pp. of text. 6⅛ × 9¼. 22118-0, 22119-9 Pa. Two-vol. set $15.90

ALASKA: The Harriman Expedition, 1899, John Burroughs, John Muir, et al. Informative, engrossing accounts of two-month, 9,000-mile expedition. Native peoples, wildlife, forests, geography, salmon industry, glaciers, more. Profusely illustrated. 240 black-and-white line drawings. 124 black-and-white photographs. 3 maps. Index. 576pp. 5⅜ × 8½. 25109-8 Pa. $11.95

THE BOOK OF BEASTS: Being a Translation from a Latin Bestiary of the Twelfth Century, T. H. White. Wonderful catalog real and fanciful beasts: manticore, griffin, phoenix, amphivius, jaculus, many more. White's witty erudite commentary on scientific, historical aspects. Fascinating glimpse of medieval mind. Illustrated. 296pp. 5⅜ × 8¼. (Available in U.S. only) 24609-4 Pa. $5.95

FRANK LLOYD WRIGHT: ARCHITECTURE AND NATURE With 160 Illustrations, Donald Hoffmann. Profusely illustrated study of influence of nature—especially prairie—on Wright's designs for Fallingwater, Robie House, Guggenheim Museum, other masterpieces. 96pp. 9¼ × 10¾. 25098-9 Pa. $7.95

FRANK LLOYD WRIGHT'S FALLINGWATER, Donald Hoffmann. Wright's famous waterfall house: planning and construction of organic idea. History of site, owners, Wright's personal involvement. Photographs of various stages of building. Preface by Edgar Kaufmann, Jr. 100 illustrations. 112pp. 9¼ × 10. 23671-4 Pa. $7.95

YEARS WITH FRANK LLOYD WRIGHT: Apprentice to Genius, Edgar Tafel. Insightful memoir by a former apprentice presents a revealing portrait of Wright the man, the inspired teacher, the greatest American architect. 372 black-and-white illustrations. Preface. Index. vi + 228pp. 8¼ × 11. 24801-1 Pa. $9.95

THE STORY OF KING ARTHUR AND HIS KNIGHTS, Howard Pyle. Enchanting version of King Arthur fable has delighted generations with imaginative narratives of exciting adventures and unforgettable illustrations by the author. 41 illustrations. xviii + 313pp. 6⅛ × 9¼. 21445-1 Pa. $5.95

THE GODS OF THE EGYPTIANS, E. A. Wallis Budge. Thorough coverage of numerous gods of ancient Egypt by foremost Egyptologist. Information on evolution of cults, rites and gods; the cult of Osiris; the Book of the Dead and its rites; the sacred animals and birds; Heaven and Hell; and more. 956pp. 6⅛ × 9¼. 22055-9, 22056-7 Pa., Two-vol. set $21.90

A THEOLOGICO-POLITICAL TREATISE, Benedict Spinoza. Also contains unfinished *Political Treatise*. Great classic on religious liberty, theory of government on common consent. R. Elwes translation. Total of 421pp. 5⅜ × 8½. 20249-6 Pa. $6.95

INCIDENTS OF TRAVEL IN CENTRAL AMERICA, CHIAPAS, AND YUCATAN, John L. Stephens. Almost single-handed discovery of Maya culture; exploration of ruined cities, monuments, temples; customs of Indians. 115 drawings. 892pp. 5⅜ × 8½. 22404-X, 22405-8 Pa., Two-vol. set $15.90

LOS CAPRICHOS, Francisco Goya. 80 plates of wild, grotesque monsters and caricatures. Prado manuscript included. 183pp. 6⅛ × 9⅜. 22384-1 Pa. $4.95

AUTOBIOGRAPHY: The Story of My Experiments with Truth, Mohandas K. Gandhi. Not hagiography, but Gandhi in his own words. Boyhood, legal studies, purification, the growth of the Satyagraha (nonviolent protest) movement. Critical, inspiring work of the man who freed India. 480pp. 5⅜ × 8½. (Available in U.S. only) 24593-4 Pa. $6.95

ILLUSTRATED DICTIONARY OF HISTORIC ARCHITECTURE, edited by Cyril M. Harris. Extraordinary compendium of clear, concise definitions for over 5,000 important architectural terms complemented by over 2,000 line drawings. Covers full spectrum of architecture from ancient ruins to 20th-century Modernism. Preface. 592pp. 7½ × 9⅝. 24444-X Pa. $14.95

THE NIGHT BEFORE CHRISTMAS, Clement Moore. Full text, and woodcuts from original 1848 book. Also critical, historical material. 19 illustrations. 40pp. 4⅝ × 6. 22797-9 Pa. $2.50

THE LESSON OF JAPANESE ARCHITECTURE: 165 Photographs, Jiro Harada. Memorable gallery of 165 photographs taken in the 1930's of exquisite Japanese homes of the well-to-do and historic buildings. 13 line diagrams. 192pp. 8⅜ × 11¼. 24778-3 Pa. $8.95

THE AUTOBIOGRAPHY OF CHARLES DARWIN AND SELECTED LETTERS, edited by Francis Darwin. The fascinating life of eccentric genius composed of an intimate memoir by Darwin (intended for his children); commentary by his son, Francis; hundreds of fragments from notebooks, journals, papers; and letters to and from Lyell, Hooker, Huxley, Wallace and Henslow. xi + 365pp. 5⅜ × 8. 20479-0 Pa. $5.95

WONDERS OF THE SKY: Observing Rainbows, Comets, Eclipses, the Stars and Other Phenomena, Fred Schaaf. Charming, easy-to-read poetic guide to all manner of celestial events visible to the naked eye. Mock suns, glories, Belt of Venus, more. Illustrated. 299pp. 5¼ × 8¼. 24402-4 Pa. $7.95

BURNHAM'S CELESTIAL HANDBOOK, Robert Burnham, Jr. Thorough guide to the stars beyond our solar system. Exhaustive treatment. Alphabetical by constellation: Andromeda to Cetus in Vol. 1; Chamaeleon to Orion in Vol. 2; and Pavo to Vulpecula in Vol. 3. Hundreds of illustrations. Index in Vol. 3. 2,000pp. 6⅛ × 9¼. 23567-X, 23568-8, 23673-0 Pa., Three-vol. set $37.85

STAR NAMES: Their Lore and Meaning, Richard Hinckley Allen. Fascinating history of names various cultures have given to constellations and literary and folkloristic uses that have been made of stars. Indexes to subjects. Arabic and Greek names. Biblical references. Bibliography. 563pp. 5⅜ × 8½. 21079-0 Pa. $7.95

THIRTY YEARS THAT SHOOK PHYSICS: The Story of Quantum Theory, George Gamow. Lucid, accessible introduction to influential theory of energy and matter. Careful explanations of Dirac's anti-particles, Bohr's model of the atom, much more. 12 plates. Numerous drawings. 240pp. 5⅜ × 8½. 24895-X Pa. $4.95

CHINESE DOMESTIC FURNITURE IN PHOTOGRAPHS AND MEASURED DRAWINGS, Gustav Ecke. A rare volume, now affordably priced for antique collectors, furniture buffs and art historians. Detailed review of styles ranging from early Shang to late Ming. Unabridged republication. 161 black-and-white drawings, photos. Total of 224pp. 8⅜ × 11¼. (Available in U.S. only) 25171-3 Pa. $12.95

VINCENT VAN GOGH: A Biography, Julius Meier-Graefe. Dynamic, penetrating study of artist's life, relationship with brother, Theo, painting techniques, travels, more. Readable, engrossing. 160pp. 5⅜ × 8½. (Available in U.S. only) 25253-1 Pa. $3.95

HOW TO WRITE, Gertrude Stein. Gertrude Stein claimed anyone could understand her unconventional writing—here are clues to help. Fascinating improvisations, language experiments, explanations illuminate Stein's craft and the art of writing. Total of 414pp. 4⅜ × 6⅜. 23144-5 Pa. $5.95

ADVENTURES AT SEA IN THE GREAT AGE OF SAIL: Five Firsthand Narratives, edited by Elliot Snow. Rare true accounts of exploration, whaling, shipwreck, fierce natives, trade, shipboard life, more. 33 illustrations. Introduction. 353pp. 5⅜ × 8½. 25177-2 Pa. $7.95

THE HERBAL OR GENERAL HISTORY OF PLANTS, John Gerard. Classic descriptions of about 2,850 plants—with over 2,700 illustrations—includes Latin and English names, physical descriptions, varieties, time and place of growth, more. 2,706 illustrations. xlv + 1,678pp. 8½ × 12¼. 23147-X Cloth. $75.00

DOROTHY AND THE WIZARD IN OZ, L. Frank Baum. Dorothy and the Wizard visit the center of the Earth, where people are vegetables, glass houses grow and Oz characters reappear. Classic sequel to *Wizard of Oz*. 256pp. 5⅜ × 8. 24714-7 Pa. $4.95

SONGS OF EXPERIENCE: Facsimile Reproduction with 26 Plates in Full Color, William Blake. This facsimile of Blake's original "Illuminated Book" reproduces 26 full-color plates from a rare 1826 edition. Includes "The Tyger," "London," "Holy Thursday," and other immortal poems. 26 color plates. Printed text of poems. 48pp. 5¼ × 7. 24636-1 Pa. $3.50

SONGS OF INNOCENCE, William Blake. The first and most popular of Blake's famous "Illuminated Books," in a facsimile edition reproducing all 31 brightly colored plates. Additional printed text of each poem. 64pp. 5¼ × 7. 22764-2 Pa. $3.50

PRECIOUS STONES, Max Bauer. Classic, thorough study of diamonds, rubies, emeralds, garnets, etc.: physical character, occurrence, properties, use, similar topics. 20 plates, 8 in color. 94 figures. 659pp. 6⅛ × 9¼. 21910-0, 21911-9 Pa., Two-vol. set $15.90

ENCYCLOPEDIA OF VICTORIAN NEEDLEWORK, S. F. A. Caulfeild and Blanche Saward. Full, precise descriptions of stitches, techniques for dozens of needlecrafts—most exhaustive reference of its kind. Over 800 figures. Total of 679pp. 8⅛ × 11. Two volumes. Vol. 1 22800-2 Pa. $11.95
Vol. 2 22801-0 Pa. $11.95

THE MARVELOUS LAND OF OZ, L. Frank Baum. Second Oz book, the Scarecrow and Tin Woodman are back with hero named Tip, Oz magic. 136 illustrations. 287pp. 5⅜ × 8½. 20692-0 Pa. $5.95

WILD FOWL DECOYS, Joel Barber. Basic book on the subject, by foremost authority and collector. Reveals history of decoy making and rigging, place in American culture, different kinds of decoys, how to make them, and how to use them. 140 plates. 156pp. 7⅞ × 10¾. 20011-6 Pa. $8.95

HISTORY OF LACE, Mrs. Bury Palliser. Definitive, profusely illustrated chronicle of lace from earliest times to late 19th century. Laces of Italy, Greece, England, France, Belgium, etc. Landmark of needlework scholarship. 266 illustrations. 672pp. 6⅛ × 9¼. 24742-2 Pa. $14.95

ILLUSTRATED GUIDE TO SHAKER FURNITURE, Robert Meader. All furniture and appurtenances, with much on unknown local styles. 235 photos. 146pp. 9 × 12. 22819-3 Pa. $7.95

WHALE SHIPS AND WHALING: A Pictorial Survey, George Francis Dow. Over 200 vintage engravings, drawings, photographs of barks, brigs, cutters, other vessels. Also harpoons, lances, whaling guns, many other artifacts. Comprehensive text by foremost authority. 207 black-and-white illustrations. 288pp. 6 × 9. 24808-9 Pa. $8.95

THE BERTRAMS, Anthony Trollope. Powerful portrayal of blind self-will and thwarted ambition includes one of Trollope's most heartrending love stories. 497pp. 5⅜ × 8½. 25119-5 Pa. $8.95

ADVENTURES WITH A HAND LENS, Richard Headstrom. Clearly written guide to observing and studying flowers and grasses, fish scales, moth and insect wings, egg cases, buds, feathers, seeds, leaf scars, moss, molds, ferns, common crystals, etc.—all with an ordinary, inexpensive magnifying glass. 209 exact line drawings aid in your discoveries. 220pp. 5⅜ × 8½. 23330-8 Pa. $4.50

RODIN ON ART AND ARTISTS, Auguste Rodin. Great sculptor's candid, wide-ranging comments on meaning of art; great artists; relation of sculpture to poetry, painting, music; philosophy of life, more. 76 superb black-and-white illustrations of Rodin's sculpture, drawings and prints. 119pp. 8⅜ × 11¼. 24487-3 Pa. $6.95

FIFTY CLASSIC FRENCH FILMS, 1912–1982: A Pictorial Record, Anthony Slide. Memorable stills from Grand Illusion, Beauty and the Beast, Hiroshima, Mon Amour, many more. Credits, plot synopses, reviews, etc. 160pp. 8¼ × 11. 25256-6 Pa. $11.95

THE PRINCIPLES OF PSYCHOLOGY, William James. Famous long course complete, unabridged. Stream of thought, time perception, memory, experimental methods; great work decades ahead of its time. 94 figures. 1,391pp. 5⅜ × 8½. 20381-6, 20382-4 Pa., Two-vol. set $19.90

BODIES IN A BOOKSHOP, R. T. Campbell. Challenging mystery of blackmail and murder with ingenious plot and superbly drawn characters. In the best tradition of British suspense fiction. 192pp. 5⅜ × 8½. 24720-1 Pa. $3.95

CALLAS: PORTRAIT OF A PRIMA DONNA, George Jellinek. Renowned commentator on the musical scene chronicles incredible career and life of the most controversial, fascinating, influential operatic personality of our time. 64 black-and-white photographs. 416pp. 5⅜ × 8¼. 25047-4 Pa. $7.95

GEOMETRY, RELATIVITY AND THE FOURTH DIMENSION, Rudolph Rucker. Exposition of fourth dimension, concepts of relativity as Flatland characters continue adventures. Popular, easily followed yet accurate, profound. 141 illustrations. 133pp. 5⅜ × 8½. 23400-2 Pa. $3.50

HOUSEHOLD STORIES BY THE BROTHERS GRIMM, with pictures by Walter Crane. 53 classic stories—Rumpelstiltskin, Rapunzel, Hansel and Gretel, the Fisherman and his Wife, Snow White, Tom Thumb, Sleeping Beauty, Cinderella, and so much more—lavishly illustrated with original 19th century drawings. 114 illustrations. x + 269pp. 5⅜ × 8½. 21080-4 Pa. $4.50

SUNDIALS, Albert Waugh. Far and away the best, most thorough coverage of ideas, mathematics concerned, types, construction, adjusting anywhere. Over 100 illustrations. 230pp. 5⅜ × 8½. 22947-5 Pa. $4.50

PICTURE HISTORY OF THE NORMANDIE: With 190 Illustrations, Frank O. Braynard. Full story of legendary French ocean liner: Art Deco interiors, design innovations, furnishings, celebrities, maiden voyage, tragic fire, much more. Extensive text. 144pp. 8⅜ × 11¾. 25257-4 Pa. $9.95

THE FIRST AMERICAN COOKBOOK: A Facsimile of "American Cookery," 1796, Amelia Simmons. Facsimile of the first American-written cookbook published in the United States contains authentic recipes for colonial favorites—pumpkin pudding, winter squash pudding, spruce beer, Indian slapjacks, and more. Introductory Essay and Glossary of colonial cooking terms. 80pp. 5⅜ × 8½. 24710-4 Pa. $3.50

101 PUZZLES IN THOUGHT AND LOGIC, C. R. Wylie, Jr. Solve murders and robberies, find out which fishermen are liars, how a blind man could possibly identify a color—purely by your own reasoning! 107pp. 5⅜ × 8½. 20367-0 Pa. $2.50

THE BOOK OF WORLD-FAMOUS MUSIC—CLASSICAL, POPULAR AND FOLK, James J. Fuld. Revised and enlarged republication of landmark work in musico-bibliography. Full information about nearly 1,000 songs and compositions including first lines of music and lyrics. New supplement. Index. 800pp. 5⅜ × 8¼. 24857-7 Pa. $14.95

ANTHROPOLOGY AND MODERN LIFE, Franz Boas. Great anthropologist's classic treatise on race and culture. Introduction by Ruth Bunzel. Only inexpensive paperback edition. 255pp. 5⅜ × 8½. 25245-0 Pa. $5.95

THE TALE OF PETER RABBIT, Beatrix Potter. The inimitable Peter's terrifying adventure in Mr. McGregor's garden, with all 27 wonderful, full-color Potter illustrations. 55pp. 4¼ × 5½. (Available in U.S. only) 22827-4 Pa. $1.75

THREE PROPHETIC SCIENCE FICTION NOVELS, H. G. Wells. *When the Sleeper Wakes, A Story of the Days to Come* and *The Time Machine* (full version). 335pp. 5⅜ × 8½. (Available in U.S. only) 20605-X Pa. $5.95

APICIUS COOKERY AND DINING IN IMPERIAL ROME, edited and translated by Joseph Dommers Vehling. Oldest known cookbook in existence offers readers a clear picture of what foods Romans ate, how they prepared them, etc. 49 illustrations. 301pp. 6⅛ × 9¼. 23563-7 Pa. $6.50

SHAKESPEARE LEXICON AND QUOTATION DICTIONARY, Alexander Schmidt. Full definitions, locations, shades of meaning of every word in plays and poems. More than 50,000 exact quotations. 1,485pp. 6½ × 9¼. 22726-X, 22727-8 Pa., Two-vol. set $27.90

THE WORLD'S GREAT SPEECHES, edited by Lewis Copeland and Lawrence W. Lamm. Vast collection of 278 speeches from Greeks to 1970. Powerful and effective models; unique look at history. 842pp. 5⅜ × 8½. 20468-5 Pa. $11.95

CATALOG OF DOVER BOOKS

THE BLUE FAIRY BOOK, Andrew Lang. The first, most famous collection, with many familiar tales: Little Red Riding Hood, Aladdin and the Wonderful Lamp, Puss in Boots, Sleeping Beauty, Hansel and Gretel, Rumpelstiltskin; 37 in all. 138 illustrations. 390pp. 5⅜ × 8½. 21437-0 Pa. $5.95

THE STORY OF THE CHAMPIONS OF THE ROUND TABLE, Howard Pyle. Sir Launcelot, Sir Tristram and Sir Percival in spirited adventures of love and triumph retold in Pyle's inimitable style. 50 drawings, 31 full-page. xviii + 329pp. 6½ × 9¼. 21883-X Pa. $6.95

AUDUBON AND HIS JOURNALS, Maria Audubon. Unmatched two-volume portrait of the great artist, naturalist and author contains his journals, an excellent biography by his granddaughter, expert annotations by the noted ornithologist, Dr. Elliott Coues, and 37 superb illustrations. Total of 1,200pp. 5⅜ × 8.
Vol. I 25143-8 Pa. $8.95
Vol. II 25144-6 Pa. $8.95

GREAT DINOSAUR HUNTERS AND THEIR DISCOVERIES, Edwin H. Colbert. Fascinating, lavishly illustrated chronicle of dinosaur research, 1820's to 1960. Achievements of Cope, Marsh, Brown, Buckland, Mantell, Huxley, many others. 384pp. 5¼ × 8¼. 24701-5 Pa. $6.95

THE TASTEMAKERS, Russell Lynes. Informal, illustrated social history of American taste 1850's–1950's. First popularized categories Highbrow, Lowbrow, Middlebrow. 129 illustrations. New (1979) afterword. 384pp. 6 × 9.
23993-4 Pa. $6.95

DOUBLE CROSS PURPOSES, Ronald A. Knox. A treasure hunt in the Scottish Highlands, an old map, unidentified corpse, surprise discoveries keep reader guessing in this cleverly intricate tale of financial skullduggery. 2 black-and-white maps. 320pp. 5⅜ × 8½. (Available in U.S. only) 25032-6 Pa. $5.95

AUTHENTIC VICTORIAN DECORATION AND ORNAMENTATION IN FULL COLOR: 46 Plates from "Studies in Design," Christopher Dresser. Superb full-color lithographs reproduced from rare original portfolio of a major Victorian designer. 48pp. 9¼ × 12¼. 25083-0 Pa. $7.95

PRIMITIVE ART, Franz Boas. Remains the best text ever prepared on subject, thoroughly discussing Indian, African, Asian, Australian, and, especially, Northern American primitive art. Over 950 illustrations show ceramics, masks, totem poles, weapons, textiles, paintings, much more. 376pp. 5⅜ × 8. 20025-6 Pa. $6.95

SIDELIGHTS ON RELATIVITY, Albert Einstein. Unabridged republication of two lectures delivered by the great physicist in 1920–21. Ether and Relativity and Geometry and Experience. Elegant ideas in non-mathematical form, accessible to intelligent layman. vi + 56pp. 5⅜ × 8½. 24511-X Pa. $2.95

THE WIT AND HUMOR OF OSCAR WILDE, edited by Alvin Redman. More than 1,000 ripostes, paradoxes, wisecracks: Work is the curse of the drinking classes, I can resist everything except temptation, etc. 258pp. 5⅜ × 8½. 20602-5 Pa. $4.50

ADVENTURES WITH A MICROSCOPE, Richard Headstrom. 59 adventures with clothing fibers, protozoa, ferns and lichens, roots and leaves, much more. 142 illustrations. 232pp. 5⅜ × 8½. 23471-1 Pa. $3.95

PLANTS OF THE BIBLE, Harold N. Moldenke and Alma L. Moldenke. Standard reference to all 230 plants mentioned in Scriptures. Latin name, biblical reference, uses, modern identity, much more. Unsurpassed encyclopedic resource for scholars, botanists, nature lovers, students of Bible. Bibliography. Indexes. 123 black-and-white illustrations. 384pp. 6 × 9. 25069-5 Pa. $8.95

FAMOUS AMERICAN WOMEN: A Biographical Dictionary from Colonial Times to the Present, Robert McHenry, ed. From Pocahontas to Rosa Parks, 1,035 distinguished American women documented in separate biographical entries. Accurate, up-to-date data, numerous categories, spans 400 years. Indices. 493pp. 6½ × 9¼. 24523-3 Pa. $9.95

THE FABULOUS INTERIORS OF THE GREAT OCEAN LINERS IN HISTORIC PHOTOGRAPHS, William H. Miller, Jr. Some 200 superb photographs capture exquisite interiors of world's great "floating palaces"—1890's to 1980's: *Titanic, Ile de France, Queen Elizabeth, United States, Europa,* more. Approx. 200 black-and-white photographs. Captions. Text. Introduction. 160pp. 8⅞ × 11¾. 24756-2 Pa. $9.95

THE GREAT LUXURY LINERS, 1927-1954: A Photographic Record, William H. Miller, Jr. Nostalgic tribute to heyday of ocean liners. 186 photos of Ile de France, Normandie, Leviathan, Queen Elizabeth, United States, many others. Interior and exterior views. Introduction. Captions. 160pp. 9 × 12. 24056-8 Pa. $9.95

A NATURAL HISTORY OF THE DUCKS, John Charles Phillips. Great landmark of ornithology offers complete detailed coverage of nearly 200 species and subspecies of ducks: gadwall, sheldrake, merganser, pintail, many more. 74 full-color plates, 102 black-and-white. Bibliography. Total of 1,920pp. 8⅝ × 11¼. 25141-1, 25142-X Cloth. Two-vol. set $100.00

THE SEAWEED HANDBOOK: An Illustrated Guide to Seaweeds from North Carolina to Canada, Thomas F. Lee. Concise reference covers 78 species. Scientific and common names, habitat, distribution, more. Finding keys for easy identification. 224pp. 5⅜ × 8½. 25215-9 Pa. $5.95

THE TEN BOOKS OF ARCHITECTURE: The 1755 Leoni Edition, Leon Battista Alberti. Rare classic helped introduce the glories of ancient architecture to the Renaissance. 68 black-and-white plates. 336pp. 8⅜ × 11¼. 25239-6 Pa. $14.95

MISS MACKENZIE, Anthony Trollope. Minor masterpieces by Victorian master unmasks many truths about life in 19th-century England. First inexpensive edition in years. 392pp. 5⅜ × 8½. 25201-9 Pa. $7.95

THE RIME OF THE ANCIENT MARINER, Gustave Doré, Samuel Taylor Coleridge. Dramatic engravings considered by many to be his greatest work. The terrifying space of the open sea, the storms and whirlpools of an unknown ocean, the ice of Antarctica, more—all rendered in a powerful, chilling manner. Full text. 38 plates. 77pp. 9¼ × 12. 22305-1 Pa. $4.95

THE EXPEDITIONS OF ZEBULON MONTGOMERY PIKE, Zebulon Montgomery Pike. Fascinating first-hand accounts (1805-6) of exploration of Mississippi River, Indian wars, capture by Spanish dragoons, much more. 1,088pp. 5⅜ × 8½. 25254-X, 25255-8 Pa. Two-vol. set $23.90

A CONCISE HISTORY OF PHOTOGRAPHY: Third Revised Edition, Helmut Gernsheim. Best one-volume history—camera obscura, photochemistry, daguerreotypes, evolution of cameras, film, more. Also artistic aspects—landscape, portraits, fine art, etc. 281 black-and-white photographs. 26 in color. 176pp. 8⅜ × 11¼. 25128-4 Pa. $12.95

THE DORÉ BIBLE ILLUSTRATIONS, Gustave Doré. 241 detailed plates from the Bible: the Creation scenes, Adam and Eve, Flood, Babylon, battle sequences, life of Jesus, etc. Each plate is accompanied by the verses from the King James version of the Bible. 241pp. 9 × 12. 23004-X Pa. $8.95

HUGGER-MUGGER IN THE LOUVRE, Elliot Paul. Second Homer Evans mystery-comedy. Theft at the Louvre involves sleuth in hilarious, madcap caper. "A knockout."—Books. 336pp. 5⅜ × 8½. 25185-3 Pa. $5.95

FLATLAND, E. A. Abbott. Intriguing and enormously popular science-fiction classic explores the complexities of trying to survive as a two-dimensional being in a three-dimensional world. Amusingly illustrated by the author. 16 illustrations. 103pp. 5⅜ × 8½. 20001-9 Pa. $2.25

THE HISTORY OF THE LEWIS AND CLARK EXPEDITION, Meriwether Lewis and William Clark, edited by Elliott Coues. Classic edition of Lewis and Clark's day-by-day journals that later became the basis for U.S. claims to Oregon and the West. Accurate and invaluable geographical, botanical, biological, meteorological and anthropological material. Total of 1,508pp. 5⅜ × 8½. 21268-8, 21269-6, 21270-X Pa. Three-vol. set $25.50

LANGUAGE, TRUTH AND LOGIC, Alfred J. Ayer. Famous, clear introduction to Vienna, Cambridge schools of Logical Positivism. Role of philosophy, elimination of metaphysics, nature of analysis, etc. 160pp. 5⅜ × 8½. (Available in U.S. and Canada only) 20010-8 Pa. $2.95

MATHEMATICS FOR THE NONMATHEMATICIAN, Morris Kline. Detailed, college-level treatment of mathematics in cultural and historical context, with numerous exercises. For liberal arts students. Preface. Recommended Reading Lists. Tables. Index. Numerous black-and-white figures. xvi + 641pp. 5⅜ × 8½. 24823-2 Pa. $11.95

28 SCIENCE FICTION STORIES, H. G. Wells. Novels, *Star Begotten* and *Men Like Gods,* plus 26 short stories: "Empire of the Ants," "A Story of the Stone Age," "The Stolen Bacillus," "In the Abyss," etc. 915pp. 5⅜ × 8½. (Available in U.S. only) 20265-8 Cloth. $10.95

HANDBOOK OF PICTORIAL SYMBOLS, Rudolph Modley. 3,250 signs and symbols, many systems in full; official or heavy commercial use. Arranged by subject. Most in Pictorial Archive series. 143pp. 8⅜ × 11. 23357-X Pa. $5.95

INCIDENTS OF TRAVEL IN YUCATAN, John L. Stephens. Classic (1843) exploration of jungles of Yucatan, looking for evidences of Maya civilization. Travel adventures, Mexican and Indian culture, etc. Total of 669pp. 5⅜ × 8½. 20926-1, 20927-X Pa., Two-vol. set $9.90

DEGAS: An Intimate Portrait, Ambroise Vollard. Charming, anecdotal memoir by famous art dealer of one of the greatest 19th-century French painters. 14 black-and-white illustrations. Introduction by Harold L. Van Doren. 96pp. 5⅜ × 8½.
25131-4 Pa. $3.95

PERSONAL NARRATIVE OF A PILGRIMAGE TO ALMANDINAH AND MECCAH, Richard Burton. Great travel classic by remarkably colorful personality. Burton, disguised as a Moroccan, visited sacred shrines of Islam, narrowly escaping death. 47 illustrations. 959pp. 5⅜ × 8½. 21217-3, 21218-1 Pa., Two-vol. set $17.90

PHRASE AND WORD ORIGINS, A. H. Holt. Entertaining, reliable, modern study of more than 1,200 colorful words, phrases, origins and histories. Much unexpected information. 254pp. 5⅜ × 8½.   20758-7 Pa. $5.95

THE RED THUMB MARK, R. Austin Freeman. In this first Dr. Thorndyke case, the great scientific detective draws fascinating conclusions from the nature of a single fingerprint. Exciting story, authentic science. 320pp. 5⅜ × 8½. (Available in U.S. only)   25210-8 Pa. $5.95

AN EGYPTIAN HIEROGLYPHIC DICTIONARY, E. A. Wallis Budge. Monumental work containing about 25,000 words or terms that occur in texts ranging from 3000 B.C. to 600 A.D. Each entry consists of a transliteration of the word, the word in hieroglyphs, and the meaning in English. 1,314pp. 6⅞ × 10.
23615-3, 23616-1 Pa., Two-vol. set $27.90

THE COMPLEAT STRATEGYST: Being a Primer on the Theory of Games of Strategy, J. D. Williams. Highly entertaining classic describes, with many illustrated examples, how to select best strategies in conflict situations. Prefaces. Appendices. xvi + 268pp. 5⅜ × 8½.   25101-2 Pa. $5.95

THE ROAD TO OZ, L. Frank Baum. Dorothy meets the Shaggy Man, little Button-Bright and the Rainbow's beautiful daughter in this delightful trip to the magical Land of Oz. 272pp. 5⅜ × 8.   25208-6 Pa. $4.95

POINT AND LINE TO PLANE, Wassily Kandinsky. Seminal exposition of role of point, line, other elements in non-objective painting. Essential to understanding 20th-century art. 127 illustrations. 192pp. 6½ × 9¼.   23808-3 Pa. $4.50

LADY ANNA, Anthony Trollope. Moving chronicle of Countess Lovel's bitter struggle to win for herself and daughter Anna their rightful rank and fortune—perhaps at cost of sanity itself. 384pp. 5⅜ × 8½.   24669-8 Pa. $6.95

EGYPTIAN MAGIC, E. A. Wallis Budge. Sums up all that is known about magic in Ancient Egypt: the role of magic in controlling the gods, powerful amulets that warded off evil spirits, scarabs of immortality, use of wax images, formulas and spells, the secret name, much more. 253pp. 5⅜ × 8½.   22681-6 Pa. $4.50

THE DANCE OF SIVA, Ananda Coomaraswamy. Preeminent authority unfolds the vast metaphysic of India: the revelation of her art, conception of the universe, social organization, etc. 27 reproductions of art masterpieces. 192pp. 5⅜ × 8½.
24817-8 Pa. $5.95

CHRISTMAS CUSTOMS AND TRADITIONS, Clement A. Miles. Origin, evolution, significance of religious, secular practices. Caroling, gifts, yule logs, much more. Full, scholarly yet fascinating; non-sectarian. 400pp. 5⅜ × 8½.
23354-5 Pa. $6.50

THE HUMAN FIGURE IN MOTION, Eadweard Muybridge. More than 4,500 stopped-action photos, in action series, showing undraped men, women, children jumping, lying down, throwing, sitting, wrestling, carrying, etc. 390pp. 7⅞ × 10⅝.
20204-6 Cloth. $19.95

THE MAN WHO WAS THURSDAY, Gilbert Keith Chesterton. Witty, fast-paced novel about a club of anarchists in turn-of-the-century London. Brilliant social, religious, philosophical speculations. 128pp. 5⅜ × 8½. 25121-7 Pa. $3.95

A CEZANNE SKETCHBOOK: Figures, Portraits, Landscapes and Still Lifes, Paul Cezanne. Great artist experiments with tonal effects, light, mass, other qualities in over 100 drawings. A revealing view of developing master painter, precursor of Cubism. 102 black-and-white illustrations. 144pp. 8¾ × 6⅜. 24790-2 Pa. $5.95

AN ENCYCLOPEDIA OF BATTLES: Accounts of Over 1,560 Battles from 1479 B.C. to the Present, David Eggenberger. Presents essential details of every major battle in recorded history, from the first battle of Megiddo in 1479 B.C. to Grenada in 1984. List of Battle Maps. New Appendix covering the years 1967–1984. Index. 99 illustrations. 544pp. 6½ × 9¼. 24913-1 Pa. $14.95

AN ETYMOLOGICAL DICTIONARY OF MODERN ENGLISH, Ernest Weekley. Richest, fullest work, by foremost British lexicographer. Detailed word histories. Inexhaustible. Total of 856pp. 6½ × 9¼.
21873-2, 21874-0 Pa., Two-vol. set $17.00

WEBSTER'S AMERICAN MILITARY BIOGRAPHIES, edited by Robert McHenry. Over 1,000 figures who shaped 3 centuries of American military history. Detailed biographies of Nathan Hale, Douglas MacArthur, Mary Hallaren, others. Chronologies of engagements, more. Introduction. Addenda. 1,033 entries in alphabetical order. xi + 548pp. 6½ × 9¼. (Available in U.S. only)
24758-9 Pa. $11.95

LIFE IN ANCIENT EGYPT, Adolf Erman. Detailed older account, with much not in more recent books: domestic life, religion, magic, medicine, commerce, and whatever else needed for complete picture. Many illustrations. 597pp. 5⅜ × 8½.
22632-8 Pa. $8.95

HISTORIC COSTUME IN PICTURES, Braun & Schneider. Over 1,450 costumed figures shown, covering a wide variety of peoples: kings, emperors, nobles, priests, servants, soldiers, scholars, townsfolk, peasants, merchants, courtiers, cavaliers, and more. 256pp. 8⅜ × 11¼. 23150-X Pa. $7.95

THE NOTEBOOKS OF LEONARDO DA VINCI, edited by J. P. Richter. Extracts from manuscripts reveal great genius; on painting, sculpture, anatomy, sciences, geography, etc. Both Italian and English. 186 ms. pages reproduced, plus 500 additional drawings, including studies for *Last Supper, Sforza* monument, etc. 860pp. 7⅞ × 10¾. (Available in U.S. only) 22572-0, 22573-9 Pa., Two-vol. set $25.90

THE ART NOUVEAU STYLE BOOK OF ALPHONSE MUCHA: All 72 Plates from "Documents Decoratifs" in Original Color, Alphonse Mucha. Rare copyright-free design portfolio by high priest of Art Nouveau. Jewelry, wallpaper, stained glass, furniture, figure studies, plant and animal motifs, etc. Only complete one-volume edition. 80pp. 9⅜ × 12¼. 24044-4 Pa. $8.95

ANIMALS: 1,419 COPYRIGHT-FREE ILLUSTRATIONS OF MAMMALS, BIRDS, FISH, INSECTS, ETC., edited by Jim Harter. Clear wood engravings present, in extremely lifelike poses, over 1,000 species of animals. One of the most extensive pictorial sourcebooks of its kind. Captions. Index. 284pp. 9 × 12. 23766-4 Pa. $9.95

OBELISTS FLY HIGH, C. Daly King. Masterpiece of American detective fiction, long out of print, involves murder on a 1935 transcontinental flight—"a very thrilling story"—NY Times. Unabridged and unaltered republication of the edition published by William Collins Sons & Co. Ltd., London, 1935. 288pp. 5⅜ × 8½. (Available in U.S. only) 25036-9 Pa. $4.95

VICTORIAN AND EDWARDIAN FASHION: A Photographic Survey, Alison Gernsheim. First fashion history completely illustrated by contemporary photographs. Full text plus 235 photos, 1840–1914, in which many celebrities appear. 240pp. 6½ × 9¼. 24205-6 Pa. $6.00

THE ART OF THE FRENCH ILLUSTRATED BOOK, 1700–1914, Gordon N. Ray. Over 630 superb book illustrations by Fragonard, Delacroix, Daumier, Doré, Grandville, Manet, Mucha, Steinlen, Toulouse-Lautrec and many others. Preface. Introduction. 633 halftones. Indices of artists, authors & titles, binders and provenances. Appendices. Bibliography. 608pp. 8⅜ × 11¼. 25086-5 Pa. $24.95

THE WONDERFUL WIZARD OF OZ, L. Frank Baum. Facsimile in full color of America's finest children's classic. 143 illustrations by W. W. Denslow. 267pp. 5⅜ × 8½. 20691-2 Pa. $5.95

FRONTIERS OF MODERN PHYSICS: New Perspectives on Cosmology, Relativity, Black Holes and Extraterrestrial Intelligence, Tony Rothman, et al. For the intelligent layman. Subjects include: cosmological models of the universe; black holes; the neutrino; the search for extraterrestrial intelligence. Introduction. 46 black-and-white illustrations. 192pp. 5⅜ × 8½. 24587-X Pa. $6.95

THE FRIENDLY STARS, Martha Evans Martin & Donald Howard Menzel. Classic text marshalls the stars together in an engaging, non-technical survey, presenting them as sources of beauty in night sky. 23 illustrations. Foreword. 2 star charts. Index. 147pp. 5⅜ × 8½. 21099-5 Pa. $3.50

FADS AND FALLACIES IN THE NAME OF SCIENCE, Martin Gardner. Fair, witty appraisal of cranks, quacks, and quackeries of science and pseudoscience: hollow earth, Velikovsky, orgone energy, Dianetics, flying saucers, Bridey Murphy, food and medical fads, etc. Revised, expanded In the Name of Science. "A very able and even-tempered presentation."—The New Yorker. 363pp. 5⅜ × 8. 20394-8 Pa. $6.50

ANCIENT EGYPT: ITS CULTURE AND HISTORY, J. E Manchip White. From pre-dynastics through Ptolemies: society, history, political structure, religion, daily life, literature, cultural heritage. 48 plates. 217pp. 5⅜ × 8½. 22548-8 Pa. $4.95

SIR HARRY HOTSPUR OF HUMBLETHWAITE, Anthony Trollope. Incisive, unconventional psychological study of a conflict between a wealthy baronet, his idealistic daughter, and their scapegrace cousin. The 1870 novel in its first inexpensive edition in years. 250pp. 5⅜ × 8½. 24953-0 Pa. $5.95

LASERS AND HOLOGRAPHY, Winston E. Kock. Sound introduction to burgeoning field, expanded (1981) for second edition. Wave patterns, coherence, lasers, diffraction, zone plates, properties of holograms, recent advances. 84 illustrations. 160pp. 5⅜ × 8¼. (Except in United Kingdom) 24041-X Pa. $3.50

INTRODUCTION TO ARTIFICIAL INTELLIGENCE: SECOND, ENLARGED EDITION, Philip C. Jackson, Jr. Comprehensive survey of artificial intelligence—the study of how machines (computers) can be made to act intelligently. Includes introductory and advanced material. Extensive notes updating the main text. 132 black-and-white illustrations. 512pp. 5⅜ × 8½. 24864-X Pa. $8.95

HISTORY OF INDIAN AND INDONESIAN ART, Ananda K. Coomaraswamy. Over 400 illustrations illuminate classic study of Indian art from earliest Harappa finds to early 20th century. Provides philosophical, religious and social insights. 304pp. 6⅜ × 9⅜. 25005-9 Pa. $8.95

THE GOLEM, Gustav Meyrink. Most famous supernatural novel in modern European literature, set in Ghetto of Old Prague around 1890. Compelling story of mystical experiences, strange transformations, profound terror. 13 black-and-white illustrations. 224pp. 5⅜ × 8½. (Available in U.S. only) 25025-3 Pa. $5.95

ARMADALE, Wilkie Collins. Third great mystery novel by the author of *The Woman in White* and *The Moonstone*. Original magazine version with 40 illustrations. 597pp. 5⅜ × 8½. 23429-0 Pa. $9.95

PICTORIAL ENCYCLOPEDIA OF HISTORIC ARCHITECTURAL PLANS, DETAILS AND ELEMENTS: With 1,880 Line Drawings of Arches, Domes, Doorways, Facades, Gables, Windows, etc., John Theodore Haneman. Sourcebook of inspiration for architects, designers, others. Bibliography. Captions. 141pp. 9 × 12. 24605-1 Pa. $6.95

BENCHLEY LOST AND FOUND, Robert Benchley. Finest humor from early 30's, about pet peeves, child psychologists, post office and others. Mostly unavailable elsewhere. 73 illustrations by Peter Arno and others. 183pp. 5⅜ × 8½. 22410-4 Pa. $3.95

ERTÉ GRAPHICS, Erté. Collection of striking color graphics: *Seasons, Alphabet, Numerals, Aces* and *Precious Stones*. 50 plates, including 4 on covers. 48pp. 9⅜ × 12¼. 23580-7 Pa. $6.95

THE JOURNAL OF HENRY D. THOREAU, edited by Bradford Torrey, F. H. Allen. Complete reprinting of 14 volumes, 1837-61, over two million words; the sourcebooks for *Walden*, etc. Definitive. All original sketches, plus 75 photographs. 1,804pp. 8½ × 12¼. 20312-3, 20313-1 Cloth., Two-vol. set $80.00

CASTLES: THEIR CONSTRUCTION AND HISTORY, Sidney Toy. Traces castle development from ancient roots. Nearly 200 photographs and drawings illustrate moats, keeps, baileys, many other features. Caernarvon, Dover Castles, Hadrian's Wall, Tower of London, dozens more. 256pp. 5⅜ × 8¼. 24898-4 Pa. $5.95

AMERICAN CLIPPER SHIPS: 1833–1858, Octavius T. Howe & Frederick C. Matthews. Fully-illustrated, encyclopedic review of 352 clipper ships from the period of America's greatest maritime supremacy. Introduction. 109 halftones. 5 black-and-white line illustrations. Index. Total of 928pp. 5⅜ × 8½.
25115-2, 25116-0 Pa., Two-vol. set $17.90

TOWARDS A NEW ARCHITECTURE, Le Corbusier. Pioneering manifesto by great architect, near legendary founder of "International School." Technical and aesthetic theories, views on industry, economics, relation of form to function, "mass-production spirit," much more. Profusely illustrated. Unabridged translation of 13th French edition. Introduction by Frederick Etchells. 320pp. 6⅛ × 9¼. (Available in U.S. only)
25023-7 Pa. $8.95

THE BOOK OF KELLS, edited by Blanche Cirker. Inexpensive collection of 32 full-color, full-page plates from the greatest illuminated manuscript of the Middle Ages, painstakingly reproduced from rare facsimile edition. Publisher's Note. Captions. 32pp. 9⅜ × 12¼.
24345-1 Pa. $4.95

BEST SCIENCE FICTION STORIES OF H. G. WELLS, H. G. Wells. Full novel *The Invisible Man*, plus 17 short stories: "The Crystal Egg," "Aepyornis Island," "The Strange Orchid," etc. 303pp. 5⅜ × 8½. (Available in U.S. only)
21531-8 Pa. $4.95

AMERICAN SAILING SHIPS: Their Plans and History, Charles G. Davis. Photos, construction details of schooners, frigates, clippers, other sailcraft of 18th to early 20th centuries—plus entertaining discourse on design, rigging, nautical lore, much more. 137 black-and-white illustrations. 240pp. 6⅛ × 9¼.
24658-2 Pa. $5.95

ENTERTAINING MATHEMATICAL PUZZLES, Martin Gardner. Selection of author's favorite conundrums involving arithmetic, money, speed, etc., with lively commentary. Complete solutions. 112pp. 5⅜ × 8½. 25211-6 Pa. $2.95

THE WILL TO BELIEVE, HUMAN IMMORTALITY, William James. Two books bound together. Effect of irrational on logical, and arguments for human immortality. 402pp. 5⅜ × 8½. 20291-7 Pa. $7.50

THE HAUNTED MONASTERY and THE CHINESE MAZE MURDERS, Robert Van Gulik. 2 full novels by Van Gulik continue adventures of Judge Dee and his companions. An evil Taoist monastery, seemingly supernatural events; overgrown topiary maze that hides strange crimes. Set in 7th-century China. 27 illustrations. 328pp. 5⅜ × 8½. 23502-5 Pa. $5.95

CELEBRATED CASES OF JUDGE DEE (DEE GOONG AN), translated by Robert Van Gulik. Authentic 18th-century Chinese detective novel; Dee and associates solve three interlocked cases. Led to Van Gulik's own stories with same characters. Extensive introduction. 9 illustrations. 237pp. 5⅜ × 8½.
23337-5 Pa. $4.95

Prices subject to change without notice.
Available at your book dealer or write for free catalog to Dept. GI, Dover Publications, Inc., 31 East 2nd St., Mineola, N.Y. 11501. Dover publishes more than 175 books each year on science, elementary and advanced mathematics, biology, music, art, literary history, social sciences and other areas.